JAGUAR XJ40

Evolution of the Species

JAGUAR XJ40

Evolution of the Species

Andrew Whyte

Foreword by
Sir John Egan

Patrick Stephens
Wellingborough, Northamptonshire

The author and publishers wish to acknowledge the co-operation of Jaguar plc in the creation of this book.

First published in 1987

British Library Cataloguing in Publication Data

Whyte, Andrew
  Jaguar XJ40.
  1. Jaguar automobile
  I. Title
  629.2′222   TL215.J3

  ISBN 0-85059-867-2

Patrick Stephens Limited is part of
the Thorsons Publishing Group.

Printed in Italy by G. Canale and Co. F.p.A., Turin.

10 9 8 7 6 5 4 3 2 1

CONTENTS

FOREWORD

I met Andrew Whyte for the first time shortly after I'd taken on the Chairmanship of Jaguar in 1980. At the time little was going right for the Company. Not only were we losing money, we were, more fundamentally, failing to satisfy our customers. Despite our problems, I must say I was most impressed by the enthusiasm Andrew showed for the Company, and the encouragement he gave us as we set about the task of restoring Jaguar's fortunes.

Perhaps more than anyone else, Andrew reminded me of the fine tradition I was inheriting at Jaguar Cars, and reinforced my view as to how important it was to get the Company back on the road to recovery.

Below and opposite *18 years of progress: Sir William Lyons with the XJ6 and Sir John Egan with the XJ40.*

Since that first meeting my colleagues and I within Jaguar have come to look upon Andrew as our unofficial Company historian, and we are pleased that he continues to chronicle our development in such a thorough and painstaking manner.

It was therefore a special pleasure to be asked to write the foreword to this book on our new car project. *Jaguar XJ40: Evolution of the Species* tells the story of our new saloon car range from its early concepts, through the project approval stage in 1980, right up to its market launch in the UK, Europe and overseas and the North American launch in the spring of 1987.

Apart from containing a wealth of information, the book gives the human story behind the new car launch, which I hope readers find as interesting and enjoyable as I did.

For us at Jaguar, however, the launch of our new car is just the beginning of the story. We have the responsibility to develop it throughout its lifespan, continually responding to the extensive customer research programmes we undertake.

Because of this, I have no doubt that as the twenty-first century dawns, there will be another XJ40 book to write — I hope it will be just as fascinating as this one.

JOHN EGAN
Chairman & Chief Executive
Jaguar Cars Limited

XJ40 in America, the market which has sustained Jaguar in its great recovery during the 1980s. Photographed in Arizona, this is the top US model, the $44,500 Vanden Plas saloon, launched in May 1987. (The regular 3.6–litre 1988 model XJ6 was $4000 cheaper.)

1

ECSTASY AND AGONY

In May 1987, the 3.6-litre Jaguar saloon — generally known as XJ40 — was launched in North America as the 1988-model XJ6.

The US launch was the culmination of seven years' work by (Sir) John Egan and his latter-day Jaguar team, and the name, XJ6, was just about the only thing that was not completely new, unless one considered the sleek, unmistakable, crouching stance that the famous feline had made its own so long ago.

Shortly beforehand, Jaguar plc (the parent of Jaguar Cars Ltd) had announced a pre-tax profit of over £120m for the second successive year. This is an extract from the annual report: 'Group turnover (for 1986) amounted to £830.4m representing an 11% increase on the £746.5m record in 1985. To have achieved this growth was particularly pleasing as it was obtained in the face of adverse movements of some exchange

Jaguar's executive management team, Spring 1987: average age, 47. From left, they are: David Boole (Communications and Public Affairs, 40), Kenneth Edwards (Personnel and Company Secretary, 62), Patrick Audrain (Purchasing, 46), Michael Beasley (Assistant Managing Director, 44), Sir John Egan (Chief Executive, 47), Graham Whitehead (North America, 58) David Fielden (Quality, 49), John Edwards (Finance, 38), James Randle (Engineering, 49) and Roger Putnam (Sales and Marketing, 41).

rates, in particular a significant weakening of the US dollar against sterling. Profit before taxation at £120.8m was slightly below the £121.3m recorded in 1985, being constrained by costs incurred in the launch of the new XJ6 (amounting to) £11m.'

Shrewdly-placed forward exchange contracts had helped to protect the sterling values of dollar receipts. Car sales had exceeded all previous records with the USA taking 24,901 units out of a total of 41,256 — a fine testimony to the dramatic improvement in Jaguar quality, since the vast majority of sales were for the long-established Series Three and XJ-S models. Capital expenditure went up from £57.2m in 1985 to £93.9m in 1986, much of the increase going into developing a new Jaguar Engineering Centre which would become operational in 1987. It was also noted that shares being traded in the form of American Depositary Receipts on the National Association of Securities Dealers' Automated Quotation system (NASDAQ) represented close on half of Jaguar's ordinary share capital. Such rapid growth had become part of everyday life for the company which had fought back from a position which, at one stage, had seemed untenable.

The fight had begun with John Egan's determination to put quality first and the new model second in overall priority. It had not been easy, for the Egan era had begun in the shadow of BL (the former British Leyland Motor Corporation) and therefore crossed the path of Raymond Horrocks, the chief executive of BL Cars, whose ideas for Jaguar were not always shared by Egan. Egan, the delegator, had surrounded himself with good

One of Jaguar's most experienced directors is British expatriate Graham Whitehead, the head of its North American operations since 1971 when this picture was taken at Palm Springs, California, on the occasion of the launch of the V12-engined E-type. He is seen (right) with Western States distributor Charles Hornburg, Jaguar power-unit chief Harry Mundy (left) and Sir William who was attending his final Jaguar new-model introduction before retiring.

men, however. Among them was John Edwards, a former colleague from Massey-Ferguson, who joined him at Jaguar as finance director in July 1980.

The thought of Jaguar surviving under any circumstances, let alone privately, seemed a long way off; but, as product quality improved and production rose, so did Jaguar's sights. In late 1982, with Jaguar about to show a pre-tax profit of £9.6m, BL argued against a Jaguar buy-out. Instead, it recommended discussions with Ford on selling in Europe. Ford thinking might have a lot to offer in manufacturing expertise but its potential influence on Jaguar marketing philosophy held no such likelihood.

In early 1983, the pace hotted up with exchange visits between Egan and BMW chairman Eberhard von Kuenheim on their respective territories. Later that year there were talks with Roger Smith, the chief executive of General Motors. (GM had eyed Jaguar eagerly, back in the Lyons days!) It may well have been then that Ray Horrocks began to appreciate John Egan's ability to handle power, as each overture was turned down unequivocally.

By that time, John Edwards was well under way with the preparation of a sale dossier. Two big questions centred upon the differences between Horrocks, the former Ford man, and Egan, whose truculence in adversity seemed more Lyons-like as he assumed the mantle of 'Mr Jaguar'.

The XJ40 had made progress but it was an unknown quantity to anyone without an ear to the ground at Browns Lane. Horrocks wanted to use the XJ40 as part of the sale package. Working closely with Trevor Swete and Robert Dutton of the merchant bank Hill Samuel and Company, Egan and Edwards concluded that *no* XJ40 launch dates whatsoever should be used as 'carrots'; privatization must come first. Horrocks took the opposite view. He lost that argument, and the later one — that BL should retain a 25 per cent stake in the proposed Jaguar company. Industry minister Norman Tebbit took that idea to Margaret Thatcher whose immediate response was, in effect, '*Why the 25 per cent? Why not go all the way?*' It is hardly surprising that Sir John admires Britain's Iron Lady.

That was in March 1984. Within six months, Jaguar was operating independently, and the year ended with all-time record sales and pre-tax profits of £91.5m.

They were exciting times, and with the external politics behind him, Sir John Egan (he was knighted in 1986) continued to amaze the business world by his management style, 'MBWA' as he described it modestly to his subordinates in 1987 by way

Right *A keen Jaguar owner since the 1950s, HM Queen Elizabeth the Queen Mother greets Company Secretary and Personnel Director Kenneth Edwards during her visit to the Browns Lane factory, Coventry, in 1985. In the centre is Finance Director John Edwards, principal architect of Jaguar's privatization in 1984.*

Below *Behind the scenes at Browns Lane, 1977: Sir William Lyons and Bob Knight discuss an XJ40 mock-up.*

of suggestion — management by walking around.

The planned announcement of the XJ40, as the new XJ6, in October 1986 was anticipated eagerly by Sir William Lyons, with whom Egan had struck up a real rapport. Sadly — for his ill-health seemed to have lessened after Jaguar's privatization — Sir William died rather suddenly in February 1985. Still, he had seen his dream of a new Jaguar company come true, although earlier he had seen his company torn apart. To tell the XJ40 story, it is necessary to tell of bad times as well as good.

Consultation with Sir William Lyons continued until shortly before his death in February 1985. These pictures, taken in 1983 or 1984 at his Wappenbury home, show him making a strong point to Jim Randle and examining the tail of a prototype XJ40 with George Thomson, then one of Jaguar's longer-serving stylists.

Geoffrey Robinson (left) *was brought in by Lord Stokes to become chief executive of Jaguar in Autumn 1973, and Raymond ('Lofty') England* (right) *retired from the Chairmanship early in 1974 when he realized that British Leyland's new plans for the company did not match his own. Before the year was out, however, BLMC would be bankrupt, sending the mercurial Robinson out of industry and into politics.*

The story of the Jaguar XJ40 project is summed up in the opening paragraph of the dossier issued on its public announcement as the 1987 XJ6: 'The introduction of the new cars marks the culmination of a seven-year, £200 million development programme... Only the names — XJ6, Sovereign, and Daimler — have been retained...everything else is completely new.'

Those seven years represented a brilliant and unexpected triumph for Britain at a time when the task of surviving, let alone succeeding, in world markets was tougher than ever it had been for any manufacturer. How had Jaguar — a small, traditional, British car maker — done it? After all, it had lost its independence, and it had lost its way. By the end of the 1970s it had lost the most vital ingredient of all: profitability.

Despite the enlightened approach of Michael Edwardes, who had been seconded to run British Leyland in late 1977, Jaguar seemed doomed to lose sales at a prodigious rate. As Edwardes himself wrote: 'In the case of Jaguar we failed to solve its problems at the first go. The product was not reliable, the paint finish was well below par, and productivity was abysmal.'*

Even as an independently-managed company, Jaguar had been prone to expose its Achilles' heel — inconsistent quality — but in those days there had been a commitment to the

---

* The words of Sir Michael Edwardes, quoted occasionally in this book, are taken from *Back from the Brink* (Collins, 1983).

customer, to help blow troubles away. No longer outward-looking, and without the motivation to resolve its own troubles long-term, Jaguar was shooting itself in the foot with crippling regularity by the late 1970s.

Michael Edwardes recognized the good things about Jaguar too. He knew that the marque had a special individuality which ten years of corporate Leyland rule had failed to dim. Even if the sheer good value was no longer there, style and engineering remained the two strongest evolutionary features. They had kept the marque alive, somehow, and they are the features upon which I shall concentrate in telling the XJ40 story. If Edwardes had not believed in an independent future for Jaguar, he would not have given it another chance. Certainly, he pulled no punches: 'Mounting losses made Jaguar's demise a certainty.'

That was the situation towards the end of 1979, just two years after Edwardes had taken over the helm. In creating Jaguar Rover Triumph (JRT) at the beginning of his tenure he had, by accident, preserved some principles of central management which Donald Stokes and Don Ryder had advocated, albeit in entirely different ways, in their construction and destruction of British Leyland. However, Jaguar, Rover, and Triumph did not make good bedfellows in sickness *or* in health, from the manufacturing point of view, and fortunately Edwardes was quick to see that a simple split (hiving off Austin Morris from BL's former 'specialist car division') was not enough. Separating the operations of Leyland Cars into two had, in fact, been done by intuition over the 1977 Christmas period. Afterwards 'the weaknesses did become apparent, but not quite in the way we had expected. Austin Morris certainly had problems but, if anything, Jaguar Rover Triumph Limited was in worse shape... Decentralization was right, but its execution was not... We recouped the situation, but only just. The situation highlighted the vital need to make the right appointments', wrote Edwardes.

In trying desperately to reduce its huge warranty costs in 1978–79, Jaguar was losing production at a rate that turned a possible profit into certain insolvency; and this in a corporation that had been running at a stultifying loss for several years already. Edwardes again: 'The attitude problem was enormous. The men on the shopfloor, and indeed many of the managers, still considered Jaguar to be elite and their own contribution to be unique... It proved difficult to get across to them the simple fact that Jaguar was not being managed.'

It must have been that attitude of the workforce, that *pride*,

Above *Robert Knight CBE —
enigmatic in management,
elegant in engineering.*

Above right *Wreathed in the
customary smoke cloud, Bob
Knight entertains his former colleagues pawkily at a private party, around the time of 'Lofty'
England's retirement. On his
right are England, a cheerful
Lyons, and past Deputy Chairman Arthur Whittaker. In the
foreground are retired senior
engineers Walter Hassan and
(extreme right) William Heynes.*

which persuaded Edwardes that (at his second attempt to save
it) Jaguar should be given its own dedicated head of all
operations. In fact, this was the last card in Edwardes' hand: if
it was not a winner, Jaguar was lost.

In 1979 Michael Edwardes failed to tempt John Egan back to
BL from Massey-Ferguson. (Egan had left in 1976, having set up
the Unipart operation. This departure had preceded the
knowledge of Edwardes' involvement in BL.) Meanwhile,
following the rise and fall of JRT, a 'Jaguar Cars' organization
had been created with vehicle engineering supremo Robert
Knight doubling as managing director, and Percy Plant
becoming chairman. Knight had by that time been with Jaguar
for thirty-five years.

Bob Knight is a man of many talents — most of them hidden.
While at Jaguar, his ability to damp out excess noise and
harshness from the motor car and his contribution to modern
road-tyre technology was coupled with a belief that members of
his staff were available to discuss technicalities twenty-four
hours a day, seven days a week. His orderly mind enabled him
to score high points in the psychological assessment which
Michael Edwardes organized for BL's top management in 1978,
and led him into the esoteric activity of looking for ways of
styling a car scientifically by using a calculator (actually a Casio
FK502P). Knight's contribution to road-car technology has been
equated to Colin Chapman's original thinking in the racing car
field, on more than one occasion.

Plant, on the other hand, was virtually unknown at Browns Lane, except perhaps as just another 'BL' figure. However, as one of Edwardes' leading economic advisers during this bid to rescue BL, clearly he had been appointed Jaguar's chairman to make sure that the factories could be put to better use before long, if they were not going to be shut down. Sir Michael Edwardes (as he was by now) still wanted John Egan for that job, and suggested to two of his colleagues on the BL board — Ray Horrocks (car chief) and Berry Wilson (Pat Lowry's successor in charge of personnel) — that it might be worth approaching Egan a second time.

After some weeks of thought, Egan accepted an arrangement which meant that he would report to Horrocks but be free to run Jaguar, where he arrived in mid-April 1980... in the midst of a strike over pay and regrading. 'I found I had sympathy with the men', he told the *Coventry Evening Telegraph*'s industry editor, Keith Read, once he had had a month to settle in. 'I could understand their feelings. But they were not out in anger; they were out in sorrow. They felt they had been let down over the past ten years. What I need from the workforce is time — time to get the best from the BL incentive scheme for them, and to get some money in their pockets.'

The people of Jaguar gave John Egan the time he had requested and were well rewarded in due course. But it was to be a hard struggle.

By the time Egan was in the driving seat, one major hurdle had been overcome: an estimated £32.17 million investment programme for the new Jaguar engine had been approved by Edwardes' BL board and the Department of Industry in January and March 1980, respectively.

Egan had three priorities in April 1980. The first was to get Jaguar back into operation as an integrated unit, not just an engineering team. History was to show, reassuringly, that few changes were made to the list of Jaguar team-leaders, over the next seven years at least. This was in marked contrast to the frequent 'reorganizations' which had occurred since the British government had begun bailing BL out officially.

The second priority was to put the existing house in order, with quality taking precedence over quantity. Taking over the Castle Bromwich, Birmingham, body preparation and paint plant would be the key to that one.

Third, and just as important, was the vital need to prepare for the future, by obtaining financial approval for the next new model, codenamed XJ40.

John Leopold Egan, MSc(Econ), BSc, came to Coventry — the

city where he had been educated — with a strong set of qualifications. Born in Sir William Lyons' home county of Lancashire on 7 November 1939, he had obtained his BSc in Petroleum Engineering at London's Imperial College before joining Shell International for the period 1962 to 1966. Further education at the London Business School brought him his MSc in Business Studies in 1968, when he joined General Motors to manage its AC-Delco replacement parts operation. As director of British Leyland's car parts division from 1971, he made Unipart an outward-looking and profitable part of the corporation — ripe for privatization in 1987 — but the policy of increased centralization following the Ryder Report made him look to new horizons and from 1976 he directed the Massey-Ferguson parts operation before responding to BL's call again in 1980.

One of Egan's close colleagues at Massey-Ferguson was John Frederick Edwards, who had held senior finance appointments in Britain and Germany. A BSc in Production Engineering as well as a fully qualified accountant, John Edwards was born in Chesterfield, Derbyshire, on 15 October 1948, and was thus only thirty-one when Egan selected him to come to Jaguar as his director of finance. The rest of Egan's top-line management team was to be made up of people who had been involved with Jaguar before, either directly or as Leyland men. Indeed two of them — David Fielden (product quality) and James Randle (product engineering) — had been with the Jaguar Group in its days of total independence fifteen years earlier; and Graham Whitehead had been the host on Sir William Lyons' last trip to America (for the V12 E-type launch) before the founder's retirement in 1971.

Egan's new broom immediately tackled the second priority of 'quality first' through the establishment of groups concerned solely with reducing the incidence of failure in new-car components and monitoring the overall quality of finish.

The third priority of planning for the future was dealt with on 9 July 1980 by the BL board, when it approved the XJ40 Concept Submission. The summary opened thus: 'This concept submission deals with a proposal by Jaguar Cars to design and build a replacement vehicle (codenamed XJ40) to their Jaguar and Daimler luxury saloon car ranges to be introduced in the UK in autumn 1983 and into Export Markets in spring 1984'. The fact that these dates were to be put back three years does not, in my opinion, detract from the merit of the exercise in any way; after all, you have to be optimistic if you want to galvanize people into action.

From the early days, Jaguar had tended to attack the marketplaces quickly, introducing new models precipitately, in order to keep the customers' interest. For example, the XK120 sports car, first shown at the 1948 motor show, was fitted with a dummy engine and did not go on sale for well over a year after that. The Mark Ten, a fine and sophisticated car, was tested quite extensively in the Basque country — but there was too little work, and too late. It was introduced in the autumn of 1961, but transmission and other problems made potential customers distrustful. Fortunately, the company's compact Mark Two saloons had become extremely popular by then, and they buoyed up the Jaguar's business during a tricky period. Few XJ6s were running by the time that that car was announced in 1968 — but the new model was so good from the start that it got away with minimal pre-production testing.

Proving the XJ40, on the other hand, was to be a long, hard grind, with millions of miles covered by scores of cars in America, Australia, and Europe. The XJ40 was going to be a real motor car for the modern age — without that conviction, Jaguar might as well pack up for good.

The only man of moment to pack up in July 1980 was Bob Knight. He was in his sixties, and had protected the Jaguar marque — and the XJ40 in particular — from predators. He had spent most of his working life with Jaguar. It was he who caused Michael Edwardes to write later that some Jaguar people were 'more concerned with producing new models and reaching new standards of engineering excellence than with managing the business'.

Having saved the Browns Lane product from extinction, it was natural that Bob Knight would want a slice of the action when it came, and he was not going to play second fiddle to anyone — not even to John Egan, who *had* hoped to make use of his valuable services.

On the very day of that momentous BL board meeting, which gave Project XJ40 the go-ahead, the *Coventry Evening Telegraph* published a letter from Geoffrey Robinson, a former head of Jaguar (1973–75) and by now MP for Coventry North-West, who expressed 'dismay' at Knight's impending departure, describing him as 'unquestionably the outstanding engineer of his generation in the whole British motor car industry'. Robinson's letter continued:

'Jaguar's success at Le Mans as well as the Car of the Year awards won by the XJ6 and XJ12 were owed principally to him.

'In my period as chief executive I relied heavily on his wisdom and guidance. He was the most loyal and dedicated of

The XJ40 in glass-fibre,
1979–80.

colleagues: a man of outstanding integrity and drive. He will be sorely missed.

'The circumstances of Mr Knight's departure are not disclosed but I shall be writing to both Sir Michael Edwardes and Mr John Egan, the chairman, to make sure that a viable model strategy is being followed to secure Jaguar's future into the 1990s.

'I shall also be writing to Mr Jim Randle congratulating him on a well-deserved promotion. The fact that he has been trained by Mr Knight for so many years is a reassurance that the tradition of engineering excellence will continue to be upheld at Jaguar.'

Robinson cannot have known of the document being approved by BL, but it was mentioned in a leading article in that same issue (9 July 1980), prompted by his letter and headed 'New Jaguar boss dismisses fears'. This is how it began:

'Fears over the future of Jaguar and BL's car for top people have been firmly dismissed by Jaguar's new chairman, Mr John Egan. He said: "I am going to make it my business that Jaguar will have a secure future and a viable model policy.

' "No-one has said that we cannot have XJ40. Sir Michael Edwardes is very excited about the XJ40 (the eventual XJ6 replacement) and the family of cars we can derive from its components. I'm sure I will have nothing but support from him." '

After commenting on the letter, the report went on:

'BL, like any car company, are reluctant to talk about models

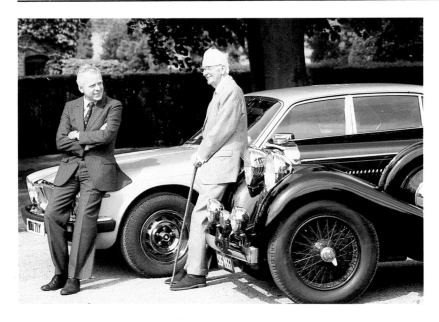

Sir William Lyons and John Egan relax during a 1982 jubilee film-shoot. Jaguar's founder and Honorary President and its new Chairman and chief executive established a bond and a mutual respect which gave the company extra strength when it most needed it.

which will replace existing cars, but it is no secret that the XJ40 has been on the books for a decade. Engines under test are already showing that the era of a lightweight 30 mpg Jaguar is not far away.

'It is also understood that subtle improvements, as well as more dramatic additions to some of the range, are well in hand and ready to be launched in the coming year.

'Clearly Mr Knight's departure was seen by many as the end of Jaguar as it had been known with Sir William Lyons at the helm. But Mr Egan is insistent that engineers trained by Mr Knight — like Mr Jim Randle — will maintain the tradition.

'Those who knew Mr Knight closely never saw him as a managing director. His heart and energies were primarily in engineering. Yet he had to sustain a managing director's fight with BL to keep Jaguar independent.

'Forty-year-old Mr Egan has taken over that fight and is now in the process of putting the XJ40 concept before the BL board before seeking cash for the multi-million pound project towards the end of the year.

'Colin Lewis, ''Coventry Evening Telegraph'' Industrial Correspondent, writes: ''Despite consistent denials by Jaguar management that the company is being prepared for sale as a separate operation, the belief persists among some trade unionists in Coventry.

' ''They see the recent transfer of control of the Castle Bromwich body plant to Jaguar as the first move in that direction, making Jaguar Cars — with their own chairman and board — a totally independent company which could be disposed of neatly.'' '

It was a prophetic story, to say the least. What it did not anticipate was Jaguar's rate of growth, which would test the new team's strength and *esprit de corps* to the full.

Seven years later, Jaguar was not found wanting. It had returned to profit in 1982, when an all-time record of over 10,000 cars had been sold in North America. The company did indeed go private in the magnificent year of 1984 when more Jaguars were made than ever before. From then until 1987, growth continued at the planned rate of 10 to 15 per cent a year; and it seemed that Jaguar's destiny *was* to succeed, overcoming the fluctuations of World currencies, and presenting British industry at its best to a global market which was receptive to an exceptional product. It was almost as if nothing had ever happened to cloud the marque's reputation. Maybe it was all down to Jaguar value and those two features that continue to make Jaguars so attractive... their style and their engineering.

In this book, I shall not embark on long descriptions of the XJ40's sophisticated technology: this is something that its competitors — BMW, Mercedes-Benz and Porsche — take for granted, and is a field in which Jaguar has simply had to pull itself up by its bootstraps. (It is a subject which embraces quality, too.) Without technology, no series-production car can claim to be the best in the world in any respect. In the areas of style and engineering, Jaguar's XJ40 made some pretty strong claims when it was launched. These areas, and the backgrounds to them, are the ones I shall concentrate on in the chapters that follow. The reason for this is that, added to advanced technology, style and engineering are what make the Jaguar marque truly special...unique, in fact.

2

KNIGHT IN SHINING ARMOUR

Several Jaguar characteristics stand out from the rest. The company's two original product features — competitive pricing and value — still apply today. They were identified by Sir William Lyons in a paper he read before the Institute of the Motor Industry in London on 28 April 1969. Sir William rarely made lengthy pronouncements, other than in his annual reports, but this occasion was a notable exception.

The long-awaited XJ6 was approaching full production as Sir William spoke of the future role of the specialized car in the British motor industry: 'A manufacturer cannot be far off the mark if it is the ambition of every keen motorist to own one of his cars. Such a situation exists with the XJ6 which, even at this early stage in its life, is destined not only to increase the prestige of Jaguar but further advance the success of the company as a whole.'

To achieve good value at the right price, Sir William had already established the Jaguar car as a leader in many areas. The original XJ6, announced in September 1968, was the culmination of his team's efforts. He was proud of the car — rightly so — and it was to prove the saviour of the marque a dozen years later, long after his retirement.

No one is more familiar with Sir William's precepts than James Randle, engineering director, who at the age of twenty-seven came from Rover in 1965 when the original Jaguar group was still being run totally independently by its autocratic founder. Randle soon became chief vehicle-research engineer and his achievements were such that in 1980 he was the natural successor to Robert Knight when he retired.

In his own seminar on the design and development of the XJ40 — first presented (under embargo) at the Institution of Mechanical Engineers in London, on 28 August 1986 — Jim Randle made it clear that his sympathy with Lyons' views was not only technical, but artistic too.

'Style and elegance have always been of central importance to our product,' he declared. 'The legacy of Sir William Lyons has been a series of beautiful cars whose style has impressed itself on the minds of the motoring public for over two generations.'

Back in 1969, Sir William told his audience how the Austin Seven had inspired him to enter motor car manufacture five years after he had established the Swallow sidecar business: 'The conception of this car had a very strong appeal, except that the body was a very stark affair — albeit very practical — as it provided reasonable seating for four people and was wonderful value for money. I believed that it would also appeal to a lot of people if it had a more luxurious and attractive body.' The first of his Austin Swallows was described and illustrated in *The Autocar* of 20 May 1927 — and it is fascinating to think that, coincidentally, a batch of Austin Seven components was at that time being prepared for shipment from Longbridge to Eisenach, where many more would be made under licence and thus set the BMW marque on the road to fame.

Within two years of introducing his two-seater — with the help of the Henly motor trading organization — William Lyons had produced his first Austin Seven Swallow saloon, which showed clever use of curved panels and two-tone paintwork. Aluminium was a good promotional feature and it helped to prevent these little luxury cars from becoming too overweight.

The Swallow company moved from Blackpool to Coventry

Four landmark cars in the development of Jaguar indivi-duality photographed together at Glamis Castle. In the background is the definitive Swallow saloon car shape — brightly coloured and curvy, but restricted by the chassis of the period (in this case a 1931 Swift). The XJ40 in the foreground is a direct descendant of the other two Jaguars in the picture — a Mark Seven and a Mark Ten (the latter being seen in its final form, known as the '420G').

Above *A 1929 advertisement for the British Aluminium Co Ltd, using the very first Austin Seven Swallow saloon to promote the use of alloys.*

Left *The difference between Austin's Seven (right) and the Swallow version, seen here in two-seater form with detachable hard-top.*

where it overcame early production difficulties rapidly and added FIAT, Swift, and Standard to the list of chassis suppliers. Soon there was a Wolseley Hornet 'light six' chassis, for which Swallow produced sports bodywork which contrived to look low and long despite the high bonnet line.

Success with these models bred confidence, aided by such Henly advertising slogans, such as 'the world's most beautiful coachwork' and 'If you can't buy a Rolls you can buy distinction'. These were strong claims on behalf of the ambitious young Lancastrian — Lyons was still in his twenties — but they would prove justified before long. Later he would take on Henly's agency Nelson Advertising, long-term.

The first car to be named 'SS' — reflecting technical cooperation between the Swallow and Standard companies — was the sensation of the 1931 motor show. 'The new SS costs

Strong claims were being made for Swallow even before the SS was announced. All four Swallow bodies seen here rely on variations of one theme: how to make a high car look low, largely by creating a false waistline.

SWALLOW······THE WORLD'S MOST BEAUTIFUL COACHWORK

Wolseley Hornet Swallow 2-seater Super Sports, 12 h.p., 6-cylinder model £220

Austin "7" Swallow Saloon £187-10

Standard "9" Swallow Saloon £250

Swift "10" Swallow Saloon .. £269

A big claim this, but who will say that it is not amply justified? Where else can you find such a brilliant range of bodies as those illustrated here... bodies of exquisite beauty and great strength ... finished in a selection of no less than twelve artistically blended colour schemes; coachwork which enables you to express your individuality in a pleasing and unique manner.

But mere words are inadequate. You must see the full range of models now on view at Henlys, or write to-day for illustrated catalogue.

HENLYS

Sole Swallow Distributors for Southern England.

Devonshire House, Piccadilly, W.1.
Grosvenor 2271.
Henly House, Euston Road, N.W.1.
Museum 7734 (30 lines).

Manufacturers: The Swallow Coachbuilding Co., Coventry

FACILITATE BUSINESS, and ensure prompt attention to your enquiries, by mentioning " The Light Car and Cyclecar " when writing to advertisers. They will appreciate it.

£310. Whether it really has a £1,000 look or not, visitors to Olympia will be able to judge. It certainly has an expensive appearance.' So wrote *Daily Express* motoring correspondent Harold Pemberton. In fact, the car was not ready for production. Moreover, the proportions were not right. Lyons (who had been in hospital with appendicitis) always blamed his partner — William Walmsley — for this; he had wanted a lower roofline. Only 500 SSI (or six-cylinder) models were produced before the announcement of a second version with an underslung chassis on 30 September 1932. Swallow's own show-time advertisement was unequivocal: 'The Most Beautiful Car of All'. There is no record of any objection to this claim from rivals.

The first four-door saloon was almost a 'Sunbeam', but when the Rootes brothers beat him to the goodwill of that marque

Not happy with his first try, William Lyons reintroduced the SSI in autumn 1932. Its underslung chassis permitted him to make the car long and low, yet well-proportioned. This 1932 motor show advertisement maintains Swallow's proud boast about beauty. While other companies were still being closed down in the wake of the Wall Street crash, Lyons' small but expanding organization was offering great value for relatively little money — and most of that value came from the styling.

A 1934–35 SSI saloon of the immediate pre-Jaguar period.

Lyons chose 'Jaguar' instead. Its announcement on 24 September 1935 re-emphasized the SS's price-and-value theme. The name itself was an inspiration; and the opportunity of buying such a fast, luxurious, and attractive car for £385 had never occurred in Britain before: in the wake of the Depression it was a winner. And there was a more lasting quality about the looks of the new car. The Swallow style had been chic in a homely kind of way; the SSI had been a high-fashion car, but its lines dated quickly (though they are still classic in the dictionary sense). But there was much more to the newcomer than passing fashion.

The SS Jaguar saloon style was maintained after the war, when, understandably, the 'SS' nomenclature was dropped, and two replacement saloons were developed in parallel by the company which was itself called 'Jaguar' now.

The Jaguar Mark Five's styling holds many keys to Lyon's evolving theme of sweeping wing and roof lines, and extensive reflecting surfaces. Its bright embellishments may seem a little excessive in retrospect, but at the time they were conservative when viewed alongside North American products — and it was the American market that Lyons wanted to woo. He had concentrated on home sales previously, but the post-war steel ration favoured the exporter. 'Accordingly,' said Lyons, 'we set out to convince the Government that the models we had coming along would command a substantial world export market.'

Among the special Jaguar characteristics established in the Mark Five (noted particularly by Jean-Paul van den Plas, a

member of the famous Belgian coachbuilding family, who worked in the body drawing office and wrote on Jaguar styling for the *Jaguar Apprentices Magazine* in the late 1950s) were half doors with chromium-plated window frames, with the rear-door window encroaching into the rear quarter panel. More shortlived features first seen in the Mark Five were the

Below *Searching for a post-war style: a 1946–47 mockup at Jaguar's old Swallow Road factory, Coventry. The flat windscreen was incompatible with the rounded nose, but the roof and tail were making progress. Lyons' trial and error methods nearly always led to a brilliant final product.*

Photographed at Wappenbury Hall in early 1948, the Mark Seven mock-up has acquired a divided windscreen (curved glass screens were still rare) to go with a more sporting front-end style which would be adapted for the XK120 sports car later in the year.

Still not satisfied with his Mark Seven (just visible on the right), William Lyons wisely opted for an interim model, the Mark Five, seen here in pre-production form, with old-fashioned headlamps and single front bumper bar.

William Lyons and Fred Gardner try an alternative Mark Five lamp layout, with the current-model Jaguar alongside for reference.

detachable rear wheel spats and the double-bar bumpers, although the latter were last-minute additions for the car's very successful launch in September 1948.

Yet the Mark Five was very much an interim model, and throughout the 1947–50 period a modern Jaguar style began to evolve for both sports cars and saloon models. Lyons looked at American cars and European ones, and then showed by explanation, demonstration, and rough sketches what he wanted his specialist sheet-metal workers to create.

The XK120 sports car was produced very quickly and looked good from the moment that it appeared alongside the Mark Five, making Jaguar the star of the first post-war London motor show in October 1948. Its style was tried out but not adopted for the all-new saloon which was to be launched two years later. This car, did however, show that a full-size modern luxury saloon *could* still look distinctly lithe. It was called the Mark Seven (there was no Mark Six), and from it and its derivatives — the Marks Eight and Nine — today's Jaguars have emerged. Jim Randle points especially to the 'rounded paw-like qualities of the front wings and the characteristic Jaguar radiator and protuberant headlamps simulating a face'.

In his XJ40 paper, Randle drew particular attention to the compact 1959 Mark Two as 'the businessman's express…an outstandingly beautiful car that clearly established Jaguar's position as a class leader in terms of value for money, performance, state-of-the-art handling, high quality interior appointments, and distinctive exterior styling. Particular note should be made of the front wings, a theme which Sir William established and was to work with subtle variations for the rest of his career.'

The Mark Five Jaguar as it was produced between 1948 and 1951, with built-in main head-lamps, raised auxiliary lamps and double bumper-bars front and rear — a fine example of Lyons' attention to detail.

Described by Jim Randle as the 'businessman's express of the 1960s', the compact 3.8-litre Mark Two re-emphasized Jaguar's unique value and low price. It was launched in 1959.

The Mark Ten, introduced in 1961, was the 'father' of the XJ range, and notable for its all-independent suspension, excellent insulation from noise and vibration, and magnificent interior design.

Randle conceded that the Mark Ten — the new large saloon of 1961, and the true progenitor of the XJ series — was slightly more drag-provoking, but '...it was still clearly a Jaguar, and Sir William's genius for holding a theme whilst permitting change is very evident in this car'. When Randle joined Jaguar, the Marks Two and Ten were Jaguar's staple products and the new XJ saloon project was in its exciting formative stages. Often, Sir William Lyons chose to study future model shapes at his home, Wappenbury Hall in Warwickshire, where the light and the shadows cast by tall trees could play on the painted surfaces. The XJ was no exception, and it is clear that he looked at his current sports model for initial inspiration, as he had done with the Mark Seven.

The E-type was as dramatic as any Jaguar before or since, and many people considered it the ultimate expression of the sports car throughout the 1960s. In styling it, Sir William Lyons had been influenced by the man who had shaped his Le Mans-winning D-type, Malcolm Sayer. When he created the XJ shape, Lyons formed the passenger compartment first, then tried a variety of noses, tails, and wing lines. Some of his schemes

Left *Throughout 1948 and '49, the search for a Mark Seven wing line went on.*

Left *The production version of the Mark Seven as introduced in late 1950, highlighting what Jim Randle calls the 'curling paw effect' of the wing, which was to be accentuated by a chromium-plated strip in a later, face-lifted version. The registration number identifies this as Lord Brabazon's car.*

Below *The 1951 model-year range on display in Emil Frey's Zurich premises, showing the Mark Seven, Mark Five (saloon and drophead coupé) and the XK120 roadster.*

seem as outrageous as those which led up to the Mark Seven, yet, like that great car, the XJ came near perfection in its final form. Its blanked-radiator drag coefficient of 0.4 may not have been a publicity feature when the model was launched in 1968 but, to quote Randle again: 'In styling terms Sir William achieved with the XJ series a successful synthesis of saloon and sports car themes, and here the subtle feline quality of the lines was matched by refined performance and a sure-footed ride-and-handling quality.'

Looking at those landmark models — especially the 1950 Mark Seven and the 1968 XJ6 — it seems that the Lyons plan was to start with an extravagant theme (thoroughly acceptable in a sports car) and then mould it until he ended up with a shape that pleased him. His uncanny knack was to know when that theme *would* please most potential customers. There is a parallel to this in the XJ40. Randle puts it this way: 'The choice for the XJ40 was either a conservative evolutionary style...or a more radical approach.' By the time the project became a serious one under his jurisdiction, in 1980, the answer was fairly clear — but there had been red herrings along the way.

Jaguar's partial loss of autonomy shortly after Sir William's retirement in 1972 became total in 1975 following the Ryder

As with the Mark Seven, the passenger compartment of the XJ6 was established long before the wing line. The E-type inspiration is clear here.

Report which led to the nationalization of British Leyland. For the next two years, Jaguar design work remained in suspended animation; then (Sir) Michael Edwardes began the work which would save Jaguar. The importance of maintaining Jaguar's leadership in its field had never been forgotten by the men responsible for design, but political issues in BL persisted in diverting attention from the main issue until Edwardes gave Jaguar the opportunity to go it alone. It would be wrong, however, to dismiss the styling themes of the 1970s altogether, even if many of them seem irrelevant now.

Until the 1960s, there had been no Jaguar styling department as such. Up to then, Lyons used tinsmiths and carpenters to translate his ideas. Jean Paul van den Plas had been brought in as a 'motor body designer' in 1955, but was never put in a position of influence. The first official styling chief, Douglas Thorpe, was given space in the former Daimler factory at Radford, Coventry, in 1963. Thorpe — formerly of Rootes, Triumph, Healey, and Lucas — 'brought up' a number of stylists. His first trainee was Oliver Winterbottom, who went on to make his name with Lotus and TVR. Three more apprentices played longer-term roles in Jaguar styling under Thorpe. Colin Holtum is a senior member of the styling department today,

The XJ6 mock-up in one of its later forms. Wire wheels were never adopted.

Opposite *The XJ mock-up with Sayer-style tail was rejected as unpractical. Even so, the production XJ6 would have a too-shallow luggage trunk, corrected only in the XJ40 nearly twenty years later.*

Left *The final version of the XJ6 tail as introduced in September 1968, showing Sir William's close attention to detail.*

Below *Sir William's 'Gothic' rear lamps and Pininfarina's restyled roof blended well in the Series Three XJ, launched in the spring of 1979.*

Right *Once the main air intake of the XJ6 had been settled, it proved difficult to fill.*

Below *Almost ready: in the production version, the decorative strip would be removed and a 'leaping jaguar' badge added. Every second horizontal slat would be removed from the radiator grille.*

The XJ6 ready for production in 1968, with a pronounced bonnet hump.

specializing in interior design and instrumentation. The fourth and fifth members of the group were George Thomson and Christopher Greville-Smith, both of whom have left. However, like Holtum, Thomson was with the XJ40 at its styling conclusion.

The 1968 XJ6 structure was finalized by chief body engineer William Thornton, whose particular skill was to turn Lyons' styling into panels which could be made in steel on production press tools — not an easy task. The new styling department was not set up in time to affect more than the cosmetics of that XJ range. When the first XJ6 and XJ12 were on the move, though, it was natural for top management to start outline-planning the next new — as opposed to face-lifted — saloon model. This was the model that before long was to be coded XJ40.

Soon after his official retirement in March 1972, Sir William explained his position in a BBC television programme 'Pride of Lyons', compiled by Peter Colebourne to mark the half-century since the Swallow Sidecar Company had begun trading: 'Mr England has taken over from me as chairman and chief executive, and I'm endeavouring not to interfere too much, because I believe it's right that he should take the reins now.'

Later in 1972 there was a key meeting between Raymond ('Lofty') England and engineering director Robert Knight, at which the main features of a new car were established. Many of these features would be incorporated in the Series Three XJ

The XJ Series Two (1973, right) and Series Three (1979, left) compared. The latter's sharp new roof-line was not styled in-house but by Pininfarina, guided by Bob Knight.

range, which had not been mooted at that stage. The photographs of the quarter-scale model of that car are dated September 1972, and they show that — yet again — the initial styling had been influenced by a sporting model. (The XJ-S would not be announced until 1975, but its shape had been established in 1969.) This clay model was made by Thomson, Greville-Smith and Holtum, who worked for virtually a whole weekend with Knight and Thorpe hovering over them. It would not fit handily inside a Jaguar, and the Austin Maxi of another leading Jaguar engineer, Gerry Beddoes, was pressed into service for England to take it to London for an all-important British Leyland board meeting, at which John Barber was the principal voice.

Since 1970, when it had been moved from Radford to Browns Lane, Thorpe's styling department had been integrated with the engineering department's experimental workshops, and it now had a studio workshop with Robert Blake as foreman. (Blake, an ex-Cunningham man, who had moved to Coventry after Le Mans in 1955, found that his creativity in metal was being put to less use by Jaguar once its last in-house racing project, the XJ13, was dropped. Running the new styling workshop was, however, a satisfying alternative.)

Jaguar's first full-size styling clay model was taking shape; the base was solid timber, and the build-up was achieved by using plywood formers, laths and pressed-in clay. (Colin Holtum, head of interior design, compares this process to the old, traditional wattle and daub principle.)

There were still Jaguar board meetings, too, and on 21 June 1973 (under the heading 'XJ40 model') it was noted that: 'It has been decided to alter the clay styling model and this work is proceeding. Mr England congratulated Mr Knight on his efforts and the fact that he had virtually lived on the job for the last

Left *Jaguar's stylists were encouraged to come up with entirely different ideas, even if they were to be used only for purposes of comparison or discussion. George Thomson holds up one of his drawings of late 1973.*

Left and below left *The first completed quarter-scale model of the XJ40, showing — just like the Mark Seven and the XJ6 before it — strong initial influence from Jaguar sporting models. (These photographs are dated September 1972, when the XJ-S was still three years away.)*

The first full-scale XJ40 clay model, photographed in February 1973.

three months.' In his own, tenacious way, Bob Knight would effectively 'live on the job' for another seven years!

The full-scale model was viewed by Lord Stokes and John Barber on 26 October 1973. It was distinctly 'Jaguar' in appearance, but with some notable changes, including the first use by the marque of six-light treatment; in other words, adding a third, fixed side window aft of each rear passenger door. 'Lofty' England recalled (in a 1987 issue of *Australian Jaguar* magazine) that the car was to have used the existing XJ underframe with a completely new body, and the front was to be extended further ahead of the suspension to give more crushability. While Lord Stokes apparently approved Jaguar's efforts, Barber told England that the styling was 'not different enough'. In 1987, England added, 'In spite of my having many times explained the need to maintain the traditional Jaguar line, he was not prepared to give his approval'. England also said that the project, specified in 1973, was due to appear in early 1977, but made the point very clearly that if it *had* gone ahead it would have been a lot less sophisticated. He went on to enthuse about the eventual XJ40 in its production form, and to praise its

This view of an early 'XK-F' (XJ-S) mock-up is included for comparison with the saloon.

This page and opposite *A double-sided clay model of the XJ40 photographed on 2 April 1973, with almost no 'haunch' on the offside but a clear indication of six-light window treatment.*

The XJ40 clay seen in the light of day, 19 June 1973.

In June 1973, the then top model — the long-wheelbase Daimler Double-Six Vanden Plas — was photographed for comparison with the second full-size XJ40 mock-up, which was nearing the form in which it would be shown to Lord Stokes and John Barber four months later.

These shots (dated 22 August 1973) suggest early use of Dinoc plastic coating, seen lifting from the feature line in the side view, which also shows a new Mercedes-Benz S-class saloon on loan from Germany.

The viewing on 19 September 1973, with Jaguar chief 'Lofty' England (soon to retire) taking a low-angle look. With him is Cyril Crouch, who had succeeded Bill Thornton as Jaguar's chief body engineer. The rear view shows (left to right) Doug Thorpe, Bob Knight, Colin Holtum and George Thomson.

Above   *This is how the XJ40's styling looked on 25 October 1973, the day before Lord Stokes came to see it at Browns Lane. Bob Knight was reported to be tidying up details even as it was being wheeled out of the styling workshop, which is in the background of this picture.*

Below   *By late 1973 there was a second full-size styling body, on which 'freer' exercises were carried out.*

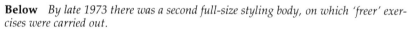

Above *The Jaguar XJ12-PF had been seen at several motor shows before Pininfarina lent it to Jaguar to photograph at Browns Lane in 1973.*

Below *This full-size Jaguar model was photographed at Browns Lane in March 1974, at which stage the styling tended to be more brittle. The Farina-like theme was clean cut and very positive — but was it in the spirit of Jaguar?*

After England's retirement, while John Barber was still responsible for British Leyland as a whole and Geoffrey Robinson for Jaguar, considerable effort was put into finding a new Jaguar style in Italy. Three Italian 'see-through' models, pictured on this and subsequent pages, were brought to Browns Lane for study alongside a new Jaguar full-scale model and existing BMW, Mercedes-Benz, and Jaguar saloons. It is impossible to say what might have happened if Robinson's regime at Jaguar had continued.

Below and opposite *Three views of Bertone's double-sided mock-up for Jaguar, photographed in June 1974. There is a typical Bertone 'signature' behind the offside rear window. A less effective but similar Bertone style was adopted for the stillborn (V6-engined) Maserati Quattroporte II, first seen at that year's Turin motor show.*

creators. Back in the autumn of 1973, Jaguar styling had reached a watershed.

*   *   *

Raymond England (62) retired in January 1974, by which time the Series Two versions of the XJ6 and XJ12 were in production, and his successor Geoffrey Robinson had made public his intention to double output (from 30,000 to 60,000 cars a year) by the end of 1975. Robinson had been running Innocenti for British Leyland in Milan, and it was to Italy that he turned for alternative interpretations of the Jaguar of the future, encouraged by Barber who had appointed him. Bertone and Giugiaro styles were shown alongside the latest of Jaguar's own exercises in the summer of 1974. However, there was little opportunity for conclusions to be drawn. British Leyland ran out of cash before the end of the year, and (to quote Sir Michael Edwardes) 'the Labour government having sanctioned the merger in 1968, picked up the pieces and took direct responsibility for its future. That the renamed British Leyland could not be saved without the injection of vast sums of money was painfully clear.'

This is not the place to go over the old ground of what

*Ital Design was also commission-
ed to produce a full-scale styling
model for the XJ40 project, but
the Giugiaro light lines gave it a
'harder' look than Bertone's
model.*

Giugiaro sent an extra, speculative design over in the same pantechnicon for the June 1974 viewing, and put a Jaguar badge on it. It was not taken seriously and the style turned up later at several shows as the Ital Design Maserati Medici.

This page and above opposite *Jaguar's own latest styling offering was brought out in June 1974 to be compared with the Italian ones. It bore a 'V12' badge. Beyond it (in the three-quarter front view) is what appears to be a see-through version of the XJ40 which Lord Stokes had been shown in the previous autumn.*

Below *A Colin Holtum drawing of May 1974. The wording reads: 'INSTRUMENT PACK, featuring electro-luminescent instrumentation with odometer and trip functions recorded by light-emitting diodes. STOP and CAUTION attention-getters flash at same time as relative failure is displayed either side of main instruments. Steering wheel incorporates an airbag, and tactile switches near the rim are used for wiper, lights, and signalling functions.'*

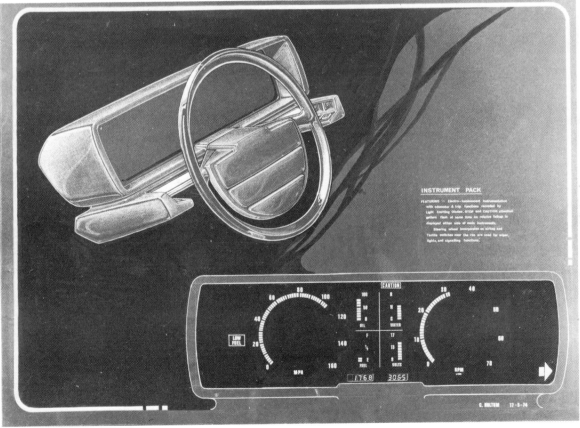

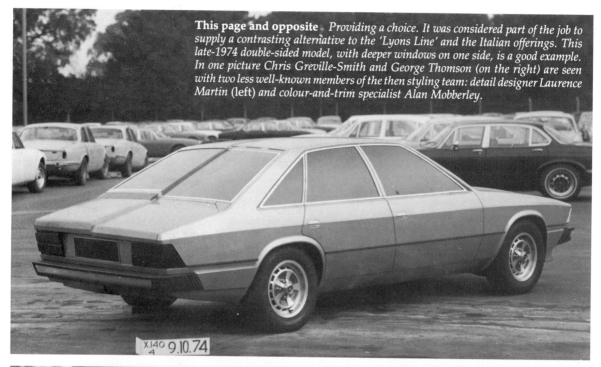

This page and opposite *Providing a choice. It was considered part of the job to supply a contrasting alternative to the 'Lyons Line' and the Italian offerings. This late-1974 double-sided model, with deeper windows on one side, is a good example. In one picture Chris Greville-Smith and George Thomson (on the right) are seen with two less well-known members of the then styling team: detail designer Laurence Martin (left) and colour-and-trim specialist Alan Mobberley.*

These pictures, taken in the spring of 1975, show how current trends and passing fashion were examined in the quest for the Jaguar of the future.

happened to Jaguar between 1975 and 1980. However, it has to be emphasized that the ability of Jaguar's engineering department to remain intact, if not independent, throughout that period is one essential factor in today's success story.

Robinson left in 1975, as there was no post of Jaguar chief executive under the Ryder Plan for BL's centralization. Indeed, only the obduracy of Bob Knight prevented absorption of the marque into the corporate system. Knight's constant presence at Browns Lane made sure that the XJ40 retained its Jaguar exclusivity, even though its official designation became 'LC40'. Indeed, Leyland Cars' Staff Director Saloon Cars Product Planning, Mark Snowdon, issued a 'draft discussion paper on LC40 strategy' on 21 April 1977, at which time the launch of the new Jaguar was being proposed for autumn 1982.

The same paper also referred to the planned introduction of Series Three in October 1978 although, in fact, that second XJ facelift would not be announced until the spring of 1979. Its styling was contracted out to Pininfarina — perhaps to avoid interference with the work of Jaguar's own stylists? The only changes to major body pressings were in the passenger compartment area, and these were most effective in giving the existing XJ series a new lease of life. (Indeed, the twelve-cylinder version of the Series Three was expected to remain in production for several years after publication of this book.)

The Series Three's arrival coincided with a major upheaval in the organization of facilities for body preparation and painting, with almost catastrophic effects in the short term; in the long term, however, the exclusive use of the Castle Bromwich paint plant for Jaguar investment was to prove fundamental to the

Two in-house models in the back yard at Browns Lane, 23 August 1976. Modellers work away at one while Bob Knight — who spent countless weeks on styling matters — examines the other with George Thomson and Doug Thorpe (right). The hard but clean lines of this side were largely the creation of Roger Zrimec: the door-handle recesses bear his trademark.

Above and opposite *A very interesting stage was reached when these pictures, dated 10 January 1977, were taken. Apart from anything else, the high quality of Jaguar model presentation has become very impressive. The nearside — probably an amalgam of Thomson and Greville-Smith styling — shows the use of strong light-lines, including a low-level reverse fold. These features are absent from the offside of the same model, which has no 'haunch' either — but it does display those softer feline curves so beloved of Sir William. Perhaps this side could be considered the start of a final XJ40 style? In the background are styling studio staff Roger Shelbourne, Ray Willetts and (back to camera) the American Bob Blake, Another American, Roger Zrimec, has left his signature on the off-side in the 'XJ' lettering and in the door-handle recesses.*

marque's universal return to favour.

Jaguar's styling department continued to operate in relative isolation and secrecy, with regular visits (particularly after 1977) from Sir William Lyons when his health allowed and, almost daily, from Bob Knight. One stylist who brought Jaguar thinking and modelling techniques up to date was Roger Zrimec. New ideas were never discouraged but, in the end, the characteristic XJ 'haunch' was to re-emerge as model followed model, and year followed year.

After Michael Edwardes arrived at BL in late 1977, there were several hiccups — as far as Jaguar was concerned — before his recovery plan began to work properly. In January 1978 Bob Knight was elevated to the post of managing director of 'Jaguar Cars' — a fine title on paper, but untenable while it was part of BL's 'specialist' car division which, although impressively titled 'Jaguar Rover Triumph', had neither integrated structure nor board of directors. Knight, however, used this period to preserve Jaguar's individuality, concerning himself not only with the vehicle engineering at which he was a master, but also with the retention of good dealer representation, the return to a factory-based customer service operation to regain Jaguar's lost prestige, and — above all — with styling.

Never, since the successive retirements of his masters (Heynes, Lyons and England), had Knight given up his personal involvement or his belief in the creation of a modern, exclusive Jaguar, no matter how long it took. So when he himself retired in July 1980, his successors had a lot of catching

up to do.

On the other hand, if Knight had not stayed the course up to that time, handling Jaguar (still part of the failed BL organization, it should be remembered) as he saw fit, it is almost certain that there would be no independent Jaguar today. One only has to consider that every other BL company lost its management team to appreciate this achievement.

Bob Knight's management techniques mystified each successive BL team which tried to infiltrate Jaguar engineering: they even baffled Sir Michael Edwardes! Fortunately, most of his colleagues at Jaguar were prepared to accept the difficult and restrictive conditions Knight's methods imposed upon them, for they knew that he was a Jaguar man through and through. His decision to retire early may have been inevitable. Nevertheless many people saw this as the ultimate sacrifice by the man who had saved Jaguar's soul and then left the way clear for a new generation of management to guide the marque's path back to true independence.

3

THE PEDIGREE REASSERTED

Jean Randle says that, if you took a slice out of her husband, you would find 'JAGUAR' written all the way through. A member of the Browns Lane engineering team for over twenty years, even before the XJ40 was launched, the quiet James Neville Randle is happy to quote his wife on his attitude to the company which employs him.

Like all Jaguar people, Jim Randle had to work for many years in the knowledge that outside influences could easily affect the company, and one potential threat came from what remained of his own old training ground: the Rover works in Lode Lane, Solihull, where he had played a part in the 2000's development. Soon after he made his switch to Jaguar, the company underwent the first of the major moves that were to result in the formation of British Leyland. Up to that time, the Rover and the Jaguar had lived in relative harmony in the market place, often being sold by the same dealer or distributor. They were 'character' cars; but they were distinctly different and, given the limited scale of production, there had been room for both in the 1950s.

The serious Rover threat began to make itself felt in the late 1960s when the BL car-makers had to compete in the 'queue' to use the facilities of British Leyland's key property, the Pressed Steel company. For a short time — late 1966 to mid-1968 — Rover was a 'Leyland' marque while Jaguar was not. In that period Sir Donald Stokes and his finance director John Barber encouraged Rover to develop its P8 project as a luxury car to spearhead Leyland's car range for the 1970s. Even the announcement of the XJ6 in September 1968, with the promise of 'new and additional power units' within two years, failed to halt the development of this Rover flagship. For one thing, the new Jaguar was not roomy enough; and it was Jaguar's prompt response that averted the danger on that occasion. In 1971

Rover's P8 was dropped at an advanced stage, and in 1972 the Jaguar and Daimler long-wheelbase saloons were introduced to resolve the accommodation problem.

In a letter to *Jaguar Driver* magazine many years later, 'Lofty' England was to recall: 'the LWB car was introduced to frustrate the substitution of the Rover P8 for the Jaguar in South Africa where 2,500 cars a year were being assembled'. England went on to claim that it had taken just six days for Jaguar to chop an XJ6 just aft of the central door pillars and add four inches to the length of the body. It says a lot for the styling of the original XJ6 that it could take such a change, and that Jack Plane — the head of newly-formed British Leyland International — reported favourably upon it. 'We got him to come and tell us why he thought we could not provide as much rear passenger space as the Rover,' wrote England. 'We won!'

Back in the early '70s, the culling of the P8 did not bring to a complete end what Jaguar people saw as predatory influences, however, and a number of Jaguar styling drawings at that time bore a certain resemblance to what would become the last all-British Rover design, known as the SD1. This may or may not have had to do with the appointment of David Bache, Rover's famous styling chief, as the man responsible for all car styling for Leyland.

It was against this highly political background that Jim Randle carved a niche for himself in the stockade that Jaguar engineering had become; and behind the scenes, as head of vehicle research, he was becoming increasingly responsible for

This George Thomson sketch dates from the early 1970s when Rover's SD1 was being styled at Solihull.

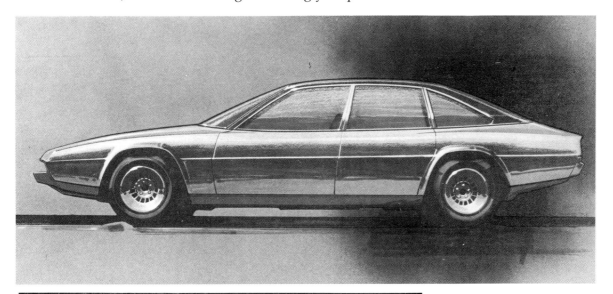

all aspects of the marque. In one way he was frustrated, working for Knight who seemed naturally to procrastinate and yet not delegate much. But, by contrast, he knew just how hard Knight was having to work to keep his department intact so that Randle and the other Jaguar engineers could pursue the course which might ensure the marque's survival.

In such an environment, it was inevitable that Jim Randle should don the armour of a Jaguar freedom fighter. One of the aims of the battle was the vital one of maintaining Jaguar's total freedom of expression. Unlike engineering, however, other Jaguar departments were in fact swallowed up within corporate ones, following the Ryder Report. Product planning was a department new to Browns Lane, and its first two occupants — David Christie, then Nigel Heslop, both ex-Rover men — had to tread a wary path, for they had to provide the link between corporate marketing and the Jaguar engineering and manufacturing functions. However, once the Stokes-Barber dynasty ended in 1975, there was an increased awareness of the importance of traditional Jaguar styling so, from then on, there was little basic disagreement as to what future saloons should look like. The Leyland Cars proposal of 1977 stated that 'LC40 styling should be derivative from earlier models... curving in form rather than angular...' and that 'ephemeral styling trends' should be avoided. This was not difficult to say, for Jaguar's own styling exercises had passed that stage already and reverted to the 'Lyons' characteristics which Barber and Robinson had tried to abandon in 1974. One 1977 Leyland demand was for 'a drag coefficient rather better than the 0.41 of the Rover 3500'. The target was 0.38. That figure would be met.

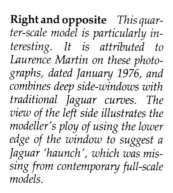

Right and opposite *This quarter-scale model is particularly interesting. It is attributed to Laurence Martin on these photographs, dated January 1976, and combines deep side-windows with traditional Jaguar curves. The view of the left side illustrates the modeller's ploy of using the lower edge of the window to suggest a Jaguar 'haunch', which was missing from contemporary full-scale models.*

'From surveys and styling clinics conducted in the UK, Europe, and the USA, it became very clear,' wrote Randle in his team's 1986 Institution of Mechanical Engineers' paper on the XJ40 project, 'that a marked change in our design philosophy would not be welcomed by the traditional Jaguar customer and it was, therefore, decided that the market place demanded a more evolutionary style, the targets being to show a clear evolution from the Series III but to have a lower Cd than Series III and better Cds than both the Series III and its competitors whilst maintaining our traditional stability levels.

'With these requirements in mind, the drag raising features of Series III were assessed using the MIRA rating method and a series of wind tunnel studies, which confirmed that the most distinctive feature of Jaguar styling, the front end, was responsible for the largest single contribution to the drag figure.

'Many other Jaguar features, for instance the canopy peak and plan form and rear boat tailing, were all good drag features. It was therefore decided that it was the front end of the car which required most attention.

'Modifications chosen were to ease the forward slope of the radiator, to remove the eyebrows on the headlamps and to give a top to bottom radius on the front end corners. These would leave the general overall front end appearance largely unaltered but would address the major drag raising aspects, without affecting the very good aerodynamic stability achieved by the current car.

'Wind tunnel work was carried out on a full scale glass-fibre model in the conventional way. As is well known, unblanked radiator drag can be reduced by fitting an airdam or front spoiler which works by speeding up the airflow in the engine compartment, thereby reducing pressure on the rearward facing areas and reducing front end lift.

'Rear end lifts are often reduced by the addition of a spoiler. Needless to say a large fixed additive rear spoiler was not considered an acceptable styling feature on a Jaguar saloon. A compromise and visually attractive solution was the incorporation of a small bootlid lip. A detailed study was conducted to optimize front spoiler depth and rake and bootlip size and angle which in combination minimized unblanked radiator drag, and kept the front end rear lift distribution in the desired range. The objective had been to improve the drag, ie, Cds below Series III, and to be better than the current competition.'

The outcome was a claimed Cd figure of 0.368...and a *most* attractive motor car. To Jaguar now, as in Sir William's day, the

These full-size XJ40 clays were photographed in the old Browns Lane styling workshop in November 1978 and June 1979 respectively. The 'haunch' is beginning to reassert itself.

This page and opposite *Even in early 1979, there were still many decisions to be taken. One side of this full-size model suggests a Bertone-style decoration (or air extractor?) behind the off-side rear door; the other side features a window instead. Alternative headlamp ideas are presented, too. The three Jaguar engineers seen in the background of the head-on view are Jim Randle, Ted Giles and Trevor Crisp.*

The Browns Lane showroom, 20 July 1979. These views show that there was still no final decision about side windows.

A full-size glass-fibre see-through model in Browns Lane showroom, June 1980.

A glass-fibre model at a clinic in Harrogate exhibition hall, July 1980.

Left and below left *Glass-fibre models (including an interior buck) at the March 1981 clinic held at historic Tatton Park near Knutsford, with alternative bumper and lamp treatment.*

latter is much more important for, above all else, a Jaguar must be pleasing to the eye.

The Jaguar XJ40 shape was nearing final approval in 1979 — the year in which the Series Three XJ was introduced — and production quality problems were grave. But the Series Three would be liked universally for its new roof and window style, which had been selected from several similar treatments submitted to Bob Knight by Pininfarina, and once the problems were overcome, there would be sufficient 'breathing space' to bring the XJ40 on to the market without the need to rush. Indeed, the Series Three soon set standards to which the XJ40 would aspire.

At a board meeting on 28 May 1980 it was recorded that the XJ40's A-post had been 'restyled and fully-smoothed' and that the information had been passed to Pressed Steel–Fisher. A glass-fibre 'see-through' model was expected by 2 July. This coincided with styling clinics held at Effingham Park and Harrogate, from which Jim Randle reported: 'The results were extremely favourable...the only criticism of any note was of the four-headlamp treatment which is now being revised.'

The next step forward, as Jaguar strode ahead under the new leadership of John Egan, was the construction of something else

Below and opposite *The Browns Lane showroom, 28 February 1980. The windows have been settled, and now it is a matter of deciding on 'reveal' lines (the left side won again), although there are still many details to be resolved. The wheels are Series Three type.*

Right and middle right *XJ40 interior, 1981. Many items would be altered for production. Here the automatic transmission selector operates in a U-gate (as opposed to the now familiar J-gate). The steering-wheel boss is designed to take an airbag. The door casing would be altered and the switch-pack moved.*

Below *1981 cars compared with the XJ40 at Knutsford were the contemporary BMW 7-series, the Mercedes-Benz 380SE, and Jaguar's own Series Three saloon. Jaguar interior modellers Bill Jones and Bill Barton find themselves the male models here.*

quite new to Jaguar: a full interior buck* within a glass-fibre model, presented to BLEO (British Leyland Europe and Overseas) and representatives of sales outlets abroad at the end of October. The buck was designed to be fully representative in terms of fields of vision and all dimensions including those for entry and exit. The only reported adverse criticism was of the seat style, which did not worry Randle since another design was already in hand and due to be shown to the board in February 1981. After the October 1980 viewing, he wrote: 'In light of the enthusiasm with which the style was received, the Jaguar Board gave the go-ahead to produce the first prototype to this design.'

In February 1981, Randle's XJ40 'Engineering Status' report resulted in BL board approval of £80 million investment in the new car, and only detail styling changes took place from then on.

Although visually different from the Series Three saloon in every respect, the XJ40 did not state its differences loudly. So 'Jaguar' was the whole effect that, when the disguise panels were removed, fewer heads turned to see the car go by than

* A mobile framework to which clay is added and the surfaces then shaped. Engineers use them to develop both interior and exterior shapes.

XJ40 interior buck, Autumn 1980.

when they had been in place!

Nothing sits on the road quite like a Jaguar. First Knight in 1968, then Randle in 1986, showed the world how modern wide tyres and advanced suspension can add to their cars' cat-like grace, with the wheels sitting neatly in their arches and the body lines stretched sweetly around them.

The loss of the 'Mark Ten'-style hoods from above the headlamps, which had acted as windcatchers and rust-traps, and the disappearance of the lower windscreen lip beneath the bonnet line were concessions to common-sense that did not detract from the conviction that this was a Jaguar. The 'Gothic arch' rear lamps were replaced by somewhat plain ones, and the tapering curve of the wing rearwards from the 'haunch' — such a feature of the existing XJ range and many of its predecessors, including the XK sports cars and the 2.4-litre saloon — was not nearly as pronounced. No matter: this may have helped to produce the bigger and infinitely better-shaped luggage accommodation.

As director of product engineering (in succession to Bob

HM the Queen Mother, a Jaguar owner for many years, is given a 1985 preview of the XJ40 by chief stylist Geoff Lawson and Jim Randle. Also in attendance here are XJ40 vehicle project manager Malcolm Oliver (extreme left) and Colin Holtum, the man in charge of interiors and the longest-serving member of the Jaguar styling department.

Knight) for more than six years prior to the public launch, and as head of vehicle research for a long time before that, Jim Randle had nursed his 'baby' all the way. As the public eulogies started to appear in October 1986, he began to reflect that, despite having begun with a very small team, Jaguar engineering had scored two match-saving goals: one had been to re-specify true and consistent quality into the engineering of the existing XJ range (for profitable production quantities) so that it no longer seemed dated in design or tiresome to own; the other had been to create a new car in the spirit of the old Jaguars but comparable with the best cars of the modern world.

Randle's engineering department — which moved to new premises at Whitley in 1987 — has grown out of all proportion; yet it is still only just meeting the needs that Jaguar was failing to meet under BL. He sees his department's work in team terms, and pushes his team along. If someone says such-and-such exercise cannot be done, he points out that everyone once felt the same way about the XJ40 at some time or another. He re-emphasized the team spirit of Jaguar one evening in November

HM the Queen Mother was shown designs for other future models. Here she is with (left to right) *Keith Helfet, Roger Shelbourne, Geoff Lawson and Jim Randle in the temporary accommodation occupied by the styling department until the new premises at Whitley, Coventry, were ready in early 1987.*

Product engineering director James Randle (foreground) and his most senior colleagues of 1987 (left to right): Geoff Lawson (styling); Mike Renucci (new concepts); Rex Marvin (vehicle development); Trevor Crisp (power units and transmissions), Raphael 'Ralph' Smith (advanced vehicles); David Tree (vehicle design); and Chris Colombo (product development and services).

This is how Jaguar's distinctive new Whitley, Coventry, engineering centre looked in early 1987. By mid-summer, construction was well advanced and major departmental moves (across the city from Browns Lane) were taking place. Full occupancy, including engine development facilities, was expected during 1988.

Exterior and interior models, as illustrated in Randle's engineering status dossier prepared in late 1980 as part of Jaguar's submission to obtain funding for the XJ40.

XJ40 project development manager Malcolm Oliver and a class of Oman schoolboys, photographed by Alex Frick while preparing a test route, using a Series Three XJ.

Jim Randle (left), director of product engineering, with UDT chief Dundas Hamilton and the coveted Top Car award, November 1986.

Many new developments and variations of the XJ40 are expected for the 1990s. This miniature sculpture is just a clue — or perhaps a red herring?

1986, when he went to London to collect the Guild of Motoring Writers' UDT Top Car trophy. On behalf of his colleagues — and the XJ40, which had beaten the latest offerings of BMW and Mercedes-Benz — he accepted the award, and with his quiet, self-deprecating smile, he reminded the press that he had not done it alone. Nor did he forget to tell of his pride at achieving what he had after working for (and having followed in the footsteps of) Bob Knight, Bill Heynes and, of course, Sir William Lyons who had given the XJ40's styling the benefit of his experienced eye on many occasions.

Indeed, the vital importance of styling is demonstrated today by the position it is now accorded in the Jaguar scheme of things. When Doug Thorpe retired in 1984 a new chief stylist, Geoffrey Lawson, was appointed. Together with six other senior engineers, he reports not to the production body engineer but direct to Jim Randle — the man who has 'JAGUAR' written all the way through...

4

AN ALL-NEW JAGUAR

'New car. Seven years old. Only done five million miles. It sounds a puzzling and highly dubious buy, but this is the new Jaguar XJ6 and with seven years of development work and, yes, five million miles driven in nearly one hundred prototypes in every possible driving condition, it is one of the most desirable cars of 1987.' This is the fairly typical introduction to road impressions of the XJ40 in a glossy British 'county' publication. (In this case, Chris Rogers was writing for The Regional Magazines group.)

The time it takes to produce a new car is infinitely variable. And what is meant by 'new'? If it means new engine, new body structure, new suspension then, yes, the XJ40 *is* new, and not an adaption of anything that has gone before. Above all, in Jaguar terms, the way in which the car is made is certainly new. Taking this into account, seven years seems a reasonable time to allow from concept to world launch.

Some items — for example the choice of transmission unit — could be left until the lead-time was considerably shorter. Other aspects of the car, however, had been brewing away quietly for years: indeed, the whole idea of considering the XJ40 as something totally new seems to be at odds with the general Jaguar principle of evolution through constant improvement.

It has been proved time and time again that revolutionary schemes rarely find a place in the luxury saloon car market. Jaguar and its rivals BMW and Mercedes-Benz have, for example, stuck to front engine and rear-wheel drive throughout their histories — as far as the luxury sector is concerned. No other configuration has yet provided a formula for a 'best car in the world' candidate, although this is not to say that this will always be so.

It is also a well-known fact that perfection can be approached closely yet cannot be reached. Perfection is unattainable.

It had taken William Lyons just eight years to progress from his first Swallow body to the 'Jaguar' car — a mighty leap from basic craftsmanship to full-scale design and manufacture. It was another fifteen years (encompassing World War 2) before the first *completely* in-house luxury saloon was produced — the 1950 XK-engined Mark Seven. Eighteen years later came the infinitely superior XJ6 which, in those days, seemed to touch perfection, and this design was loved even more in its old age than in its prime.

Jaguar engineering is all about narrowing the gap between the imperfect and the perfect; and in the past it had seemed, on occasion, that time was no object. But hindsight makes it clear that the time was not being wasted. Along with its special style, Jaguar was hanging on grimly to its other hallmark — engineering perfectionism. The key to the time capsule, in which the XJ40 had been imprisoned, was turned on 9 July 1980, some three months after John Egan's appointment. Approval to put a full programme submission to the BL Investment Panel later in that year — when engineering had achieved several targets — was given in this form: 'Jaguar Cars Ltd propose the XJ40 concept as the optimum product action in the luxury car sector...'

The wording of this approval conveyed a supremely important message — once and for all, the alternative projects had been turned down. Earlier there had been three evaluations, one resulting in the final rejection of a Rover 'SD1' derivative which would have finished Jaguar as a marque; another was a £46 million 're-skinning' of the existing XJ range (already in its third series), with 'minor revisions' including a repositioned fuel tank and the installation of the AJ6 engine which had already been signed off. This too, was rejected in favour of spending an estimated £74.4 million on Project XJ40.

Final ratification was still needed, but at least the project now had a shape. In January 1981, Jim Randle and his team produced a document entitled 'XJ Engineering Status'. Since the concept approval stage six months earlier, there had been several principle engineering achievements:

September 1980:	Prototype schedules issued.
October 1980:	Body structure design signed off to PS-F; interior styling completed.
November 1980:	General approval of interior styling and completion of AJ6 engine and GM200R gearbox assembly.

December 1980:	Body skin panel design signed off to PS-F; issue of timing release schedules; first semi-engineered prototype 40 mph crash; completion of sufficient drawings to finish first running prototype; aerodynamic testing of glass-fibre body with representative under-structure, cooling system, etc.
January 1981:	Completion of first fully-engineered front and rear suspensions; second semi-engineered prototype 40 mph crash.

Besides detailed technical coverage, this significant document also included a full project management plan, plus sections devoted to manpower, engineering facilities, and future models (beyond XJ40). Here was clear proof that Jaguar was not just going to survive but was accelerating quickly into the modern world. Randle knew that unless he could strengthen his department, and plan for a complete new engineering centre, Jaguar could not hope to capitalize on the opportunity that John Egan's arrival had provided.

The Randle document of January 1981 speeded up official approval of XJ40 — by the BL board in February and finally by the Department of Industry on 6 April. On 27 April the product policy letter was issued, and on Sunday 19 July 1981, the initial prototype was driven for the first time at midday.

Browns Lane, mid-July 1981; Jim Randle drives the XJ40 round the works for the first time.

'Actually, it was two minutes to twelve because I'd set noon as the absolute deadline,' Randle recalls. 'Yes, it did drive quite well that day; but it didn't take us long to realize it wasn't *quite* right in every way.' Randle still smiles at the satisfaction that day gave him. The following day, initial engineering release was given for the XJ40's complete body structure.

The progress of the company, and of the XJ40 programme, from 1982 to 1987, is covered in another chapter. However, for the record, here are some of the main XJ40 milestones of the period:

July 1981: First semi-engineered prototype (SEP) built, and driven.

April 1982: Fifth and final SEP built.

August 1982: First fully-engineered prototype (FEP) built.

January 1983: First FEP durability running in Canada.

June 1983: Pilot-build facility completed and build of first four specially-designated vehicles (SDVs) begun. First FEP durability running in Arizona and at Nardo, Italy.

August 1983: 3.6 engine released to production.

October 1983: 2.9 engine released to production.

November 1983: Eighteenth FEP completed. (Two more would be made in 1984: one for sign-off tests, the other to replace FEP4, written off in North American testing.) First SDV durability running in Canada. FEP pavé test begun — to continue until March 1984.

January 1984: First FEP/SDV durability running in Australia. XJ40 engineering released to production.

April 1984: First SDV durability running at Nardo.

August 1984: Completion of Phase 1 SDV build (121 cars).

October 1984: Completion of Phase 2 SDV build (19 cars).

February 1985: First SDV durability running in Arizona.

March 1985: Completion of Phases 3 and 4 SDV build (34 + 4 cars).

April 1985: One million miles of testing completed in Australia.

July 1985: Completion of Phases 5 and 6 SDV build (23 + 31 cars).

December 1985:	500,000 miles of high-speed testing completed at Nardo (Italy). Pilot build begins.
May 1986:	One million miles of testing completed in Arizona.
June 1986:	Completion of Phases 7 and 8 SDV build (37 + 127) makes a total of 400 specially-designated pilot-build vehicles. John Egan knighted.
July 1986:	Volume production begins, with change-over of one production line.
August 1986:	Final engineering/quality sign-off to sales department. First press preview of XJ40 at seminar at Institution of Mechanical Engineers, London.
September 1986:	Participation in press launch, Scotland.
October 1986:	Announcement and UK market launch.
November 1986:	Jim Randle receives GOMW/UDT 'Top Car' '87 award.
December 1986:	Record production for third year in succession.
January 1987:	Volume production of XJ40 for North American specification begins.
February 1987:	Press launch of XJ40 in Australia.
March 1987:	Press launch of XJ40 in North America.
April 1987:	Press launch of XJ40 in Japan. Seventh anniversary of Sir John Egan's arrival. Last XK engined Series Three produced.
May 1987:	First availability of XJ40 on North American market, as a 1988 model.
July 1987:	XJ40 in full production as Jaguar's six-cylinder saloon for world markets, six years after it was first driven, and seven years after agreement of the programme.

No broad description of a motor car can do more than provide a glimpse of the engineering development that has gone into it.

The material first presented at the Institution of Mechanical Engineers, London, on 28 August 1986 by Jim Randle and members of his staff forms a basis for the feature list with which this chapter ends, although I have inserted historical material here and there to add some perspective. Many aspects of the XJ40 represent a superhuman leap forward for a company which had not been in a position to keep pace with the worthier opposition — mainly from Germany — so I have avoided getting too excited about some of these advances which were necessary simply to make Jaguar competitive again. The fact that the XJ40 outshines that opposition on so many counts is, I believe, due more to traditional doggedness and resolve than to any major new discovery or invention. The single most typical example of this characteristic is, I think, best reflected in Jim Randle's rear suspension design.

Jaguar's dramatic recovery and its constant evolution are illustrated on the following pages selectively and alphabetically — and, I hope, in a way that underlines the special nature of the beast.

AERODYNAMICS
Detail attention was paid to improving the drag coefficient of the XJ40 by comparison with the Series Three XJ range, largely by smoothing the front end contours — notably the windscreen pillars — and removing the headlamp 'eyebrows' which had been a feature of all new Jaguar saloons since the Mark Ten of 1961. All the surfaces of the car were looked at closely but, apart from a small air dam in front and the hint of a lip to the boot lid, nothing was introduced that could be said to dilute the characteristic Jaguar lines. Maximum stability and minimum wind noise were considered much more important than reducing straight-line drag, although this last was improved by twelfth-hour detail changes to the wheeltrims.

One consolation for having to retain a fairly high bonnet-line (besides its positive effect on Jaguar saloon-car styling) is that the centre of pressure does not creep too far forward, as it does on some vehicles with low-drag front ends. The Series Three is one of the best cars in respect of crosswind response, and Jaguar claims that the XJ40 matches it. Jim Randle's team may well want to seek new ways of reducing the Cd (drag coefficient) figures in future; meanwhile they can take comfort in the XJ40's prodigious stability. It is noteworthy that the test cars, with their 'flying buttress' disguise panels, handled especially well because the centre of pressure was further back.

Retrospective
Side-wind stability on the Mulsanne Straight at Le Mans was one of

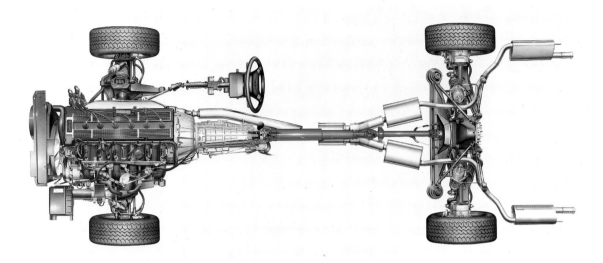

Above *Mechanical layout for the XJ40 production model (3.6-litre automatic).*

Left *XJ40 laid bare, in its first production form.*

the main features of the 1954 D-type Jaguar. Its shape (the work of Malcolm Sayer) affected the E-type and other roadgoing cars. Sayer was the only man to have any great influence on Lyon's styling treatments in the 1960s.

AIR-CONDITIONING

The XJ40's air-conditioning system incorporates humidity control, as well as accurate controls of temperature and air flow. Another feature is solar heat compensation, regulated by a sensor on top of the facia.

Retrospective
The 1939 SS Jaguar had what was described erroneously as air-conditioning, simply because it brought in fresh air rather than using what was in the car already. It was ahead of its rivals, but Britain was behind the times generally. In recent years, however, there has been a long and close period of cooperation between Jaguar and Delanair, and this is reflected in the sophistication of the XJ40's system.

AJ ENGINE FAMILY

The AJ6 engine was conceived in the context of two-valve, four-valve and diesel alternatives. There have been 'AJ4' and 'AJ5' variations — the latter being a five-cylinder 2.4-litre to 3-litre unit under consideration (in 1980) for some compact model of the more distant future (*See ENGINES*).

ANTILOCK BRAKING SYSTEM

The option of an antilock braking system (ABS) was proposed in the XJ40 'Engineering Status' document prepared in late 1980, when development work was being undertaken with Lucas/Girling and Bosch on a competitive basis. The latter's system was already a little ahead on technology, however, and was adopted. ABS is fitted as standard on the top models.

Retrospective
The Dunlop 'Maxaret' braking system was being tried for automotive use on a Jaguar Mark Seven saloon in the 1950s.

AUTOMATIC TRANSMISSION

The ZF type 4HP22 epicyclic gearbox was selected quite late in the XJ40 programme, after a great deal of competitive development. Its third ratio is equivalent to direct drive, and a lock-up clutch operates on fourth (0.73 to 1) for economic cruising.

Retrospective
Jaguar was one of the first British marques to have automatic transmission, for export only, from early 1953. Borg Warner units were specified from the outset. The first change of supplier came in April 1977, when the Series Two XJ12 range was switched to the GM400 — General Motors' latest 'Hydramatic'.

'It was originally intended to specify the Borg Warner Model 85,' wrote Jim Randle in 1980, in his XJ40 status report. 'When Borg Warner decided to terminate the development of the transmission, alternative sources were investigated. Four examples of the GM transmission have been received, one of which is running in an XJ-S. One disadvantage is that the torque converter housing is integral with the transmission casing and consequently a special adaptor plate is necessary to connect it to the AJ6 engine. Both Ford and ZF are now offering transmissions with torque converter housings designed to meet our requirements. Both these options are being pursued, in case tests indicate that the GM design can be improved upon.'

The XJ40 Concept Submission refers to a 'GM200 or equivalent four-speed automatic transmission with torque converter lock-up'. The subsequent XJ40 Programme Submission indicates that the two units under consideration were the GM200 and a ZF unit. It was not until 1983 that the final decision was taken to go for the ZF — largely, it seems, because the GM200 was taking longer to develop. It was a near-miss for General Motors!

BODYWORK
Seven criteria had to be met in the design of the new body. The XJ40 had to be:

1. *quite* new, with *no* Series Three parts worked-in;
2. aerodynamically stable while retaining the Jaguar look;
3. similar in size to, but more spacious than, the Series Three *inside*;
4. lighter in weight;
5. as quiet and refined as the Series Three — preferably more so;
6. better protected against corrosion;
7. outstanding in terms of paint quality and finish.

At 822 lb (373 kg) the body-in-white turned out 18 lb (8 kg) lighter than the Series Three. Its extensive protection includes hot-wax injection of all box sections. All major skin panel formers with the exception of the front wing panels were completed by December 1980, and most of the panels were received from Airflow Streamlines in January 1981 to permit

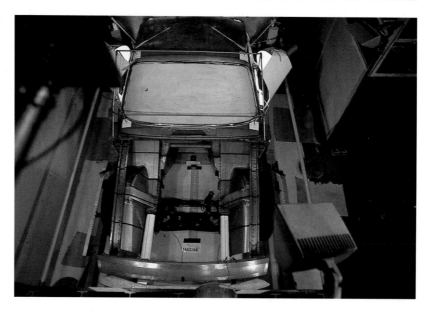

assembly of the first of five semi-engineered prototypes in
February. (The XJ40 project was moving ahead quickly at this
stage.) Ease of assembly and reduction in components were two
of the major requirements. The XJ40 has 136 fewer pressings
than the Series Three — a 25 per cent reduction. A one-piece
('mono') side, which includes the door apertures, replaces the
twenty pressings of the Series Three. Birmingham University
Automotive Engineering Centre assisted in the XJ40
development programme through the introduction of structural
dynamic performance standards to analyse and monitor noise
and vibration through the body structure: this modal analysis is
said to have made a 'significant contribution' to the XJ40's
exceptionally low noise levels.

Retrospective
*The company's earliest car bodies were 'coachbuilt' over timber
framework from 1927 to 1937. Steel pressings were used for the 1938
model-year saloons, and for a time the company owned its own body
plant (Motor Panels). The first important piece of integral body
construction was the centre-section of the 1954 Jaguar D-type
competition model. A fully-integral structure was adopted by Jaguar in
1955 for its 2.4 saloon.*

BRAKES
Apart from the availability of ABS (*see ANTILOCK BRAKING
SYSTEM*), the main change to be found on the XJ40 is the
outboard mounting of the rear discs which are 10.9 in (278 mm)

in diameter. The front discs are 11.6 in (295 mm) in diameter and ventilated. Traditionally, Jaguars with all-independent suspension have had their rear brake discs mounted inboard. This was a purist's policy and Bob Knight is a purist in the true sense of the word. Outboard rear brakes were Randle's choice; at first there was a concern that the reduced unsprung weight could produce a handling problem. This proved unfounded however, and the improved cooling and serviceability of the new location are welcome bonuses.

Retrospective
Jaguar and Dunlop first cooperated on disc-brake development for motor cars in 1950 or 1951, and used the system regularly in racing from 1952, on the Jaguar XK120C. Its successor, the D-type, had disc brakes all round as standard (eighty-seven of these cars were built between 1954 and 1956). The XK150 road-going sports cars of May 1957 also had four-wheel disc brakes — as did all new-model Jaguars from then on. The rear discs moved inboard in 1961 for the E-type and Mark Ten, with the coming of IRS as a series-production feature.

CRUSH TUBES
These items were central to the successful introduction of the Project XJ40 as a Jaguar car — quite apart from the indispensable ability of the high-performance car manufacturer to provide passenger protection well beyond the call of legislation. Back in the 1970s, Jaguar engineering chief Bob Knight made sure that the front 'crushable' zone of the XJ40's structure would not accept the Rover V8 engine. He was assisted tactfully by Mark Snowdon (*see PRODUCT PLANNING*) but the penalty was that the XJ40 could not take Jaguar's existing V12 engine either. This did not seem to matter too much at the time but, once the engine was no longer dismissed as a dead design (thanks to the increased popularity of the XJ-S model, and the more recent promise of BMW introducing a V12 engine) Jaguar went on to develop a super V12-powered version of the XJ40 for the 1990s.

DESIGN AND DEVELOPMENT
The concentration of XJ40 design and development began in the winter of 1979–80, when a firm commitment was entered into by Jim Randle with the Park Sheet Metal Company to finalize the body shape and structure. Shortly afterwards, finance for the engine programme was approved by BL and the government. The second contribution — for the XJ40 production programme itself — followed in early 1981, by which time Jaguar had John Egan as its appointed leader. As time

went on, many new features were funded, to bring previously under-invested facilities up to date and on a par with the opposition.

Design and development never stop, of course, and many more variations on the XJ40 theme can be expected — thanks to proper investment in staffing and in the latest computer and other technology. A completely new Jaguar design, research and development centre at Whitley, Coventry, became operational in 1987. However had there *not* been an XJ40 Project throughout the 1970s, the Jaguar car might have had no future at all.

DIESEL ENGINE OPTION

The pre-concept proposal of 1977 (*see PRODUCT PLANNING*) did not indicate any interest in a diesel-engined Jaguar. As BMW, Mercedes-Benz and other luxury car makers turned towards the idea, however, so did BL — or, rather, JRT (Jaguar, Rover Triumph) — and in 1979 a diesel version of the NJ6 (New Jaguar 6), later AJ6, engine was proposed for future development. It is interesting to note that the 3.6-litre AJ6 engine's bore and stroke of 91 and 92 mm coincide with those of the Mercedes-Benz automotive diesel, and Harry Mundy has indicated that the late-'70s change to these dimensions was intentional. (Jaguar had never delved deeply into the black art of diesel engine combustion, and Mundy's thought was that it might be possible for Jaguar to learn more quickly if it adopted a proved set of basic dimensions.) Four- and five-cylinder units could have followed.

The idea of an in-house diesel was included in Product Planning's AJ6 engine submission of 1979, but not in the XJ40 submission of 1980. (Mundy retired in March of that year.) However, Jaguar's 'Engineering Status' report of winter 1980/81 includes the comment that 'design studies are proceeding for a diesel version of the AJ6 engine and discussions have been held with Perkins, Ricardo and AVL with respect to whether a direct or indirect injection concept should be adopted.'

Meanwhile, two turbocharged 3.6-litre VM diesels were on test at Browns Lane, and two more were reported en route from the Italian manufacturers. This exercise was Jaguar's response to the anticipated needs of North America, where there was a strong tendency towards the use of diesel engines. This tendency was reflected in an unwavering lobby from Jaguar Cars Inc — sellers of more than half of all Browns Lane production — and work on various projects aimed at meeting

Sir John Egan's requirement (that a Jaguar diesel must perform comparably with existing engines, *and* be more economical) was proceeding in the late 1980s, albeit on a low priority in terms of expectation.

Retrospective
The Jaguar Group used proprietary diesel engines in the 1960s, but only for Daimler, Guy, and Coventry Climax commercial/industrial vehicles.

DIAGNOSTIC SYSTEM
A new approach to servicing was necessary for the XJ40, because of its sophisticated microprocessor-controlled electrical system. In their contribution to the 1986 Institution of Mechanical Engineers XJ40 seminar, Mark Andrews and David Clarke summed up the new JDS (Jaguar Diagnostic System) as a unique aid for Jaguar dealers, providing 'common skill levels for all dealerships, ease of update through the supply of latest software on a floppy disc, a high level of certainty in diagnosing potentially-complex faults accurately and efficiently, and a test station able to supply a longterm solution to diagnosis taking account of Jaguar's longterm model plan'.

Claimed by Jaguar to be the most advanced fault diagnosing system ever presented by a major manufacturer to its worldwide dealer network, the JDS data-bases were structured with language translation in mind. Initial screen texts were available in Dutch, English, French, German, Italian and Spanish. The system was devised and produced for Jaguar by Cirrus, a Manchester subsidiary of the American GenRad Corporation.

DRIVER INFORMATION
The XJ40's interior reflects the need (revealed frequently at Jaguar clinics and elsewhere) to blend traditional materials, such as wood veneer and leather, with easy interpretation and operation of the many functions in the driver's control. From the start of serious XJ40 development, the adoption of earthline switching was selected to ensure that, in most cases, simple low-current capacity switches would be used. This guaranteed the reliability that had been notoriously absent in some electrical components supplied for the Series Two and early Series Three ranges. Jaguar Engineering demanded that, where possible, switches would be assembled in modules, pre-wired and pre-tested using high-quality locking connectors. Lucas and AB Electronics were to be the main companies involved.

DURABILITY TESTING

The covering of some ten million kilometres in testing was just one way of proving — if proof were needed — that Jaguar's bid for supremacy could not be more serious. Of course, individual components were subjected to exhaustive rig testing, and suppliers had to achieve strict quality-control targets.

Mechanical targets included the ability to cover 25,000 miles (40,000 km) of near flat-out motoring at the Nardo high-speed test centre in Southern Italy. The new car had to be able to withstand 35,000 miles (56,000 km) on the 'third world' test circuit at BL Technology's Gaydon, Warwickshire, proving ground, and 1,250 miles (2,000 km) on the brutal MIRA, Nuneaton, pavé track.

The engine had to complete 400 hours of the arduous BL Technology test cycle. The car had to run perfectly in temperatures from $-30°$ to $+52°C$, and to be able to operate at down to $-40°C$.

Test targets were turned into specifications, for both internal Jaguar use and for suppliers. Engineers drew up Jaguar performance specifications which, as well as setting out how parts should work, laid down the processes component manufacturers should maintain to achieve the required quality and reliability standards. By the same token, suppliers were given the opportunity to record their approval of how Jaguar

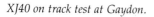

XJ40 on track test at Gaydon.

made use of their components.

Aircraft industry style 'failure modes and effects analysis' was undertaken of all working parts. This examined how parts could fail, and the measures that should be taken to eliminate failure.

By launch day, prototypes had undergone approximately 5.5 million miles of testing, ranging from the gruelling winter cold of Timmins in Northern Ontario in Canada, to the summer heat of Phoenix, Arizona, where it reaches up to 50°C (122° F) at midday. A permanent Jaguar facility was set up in Phoenix by Richard Cresswell, and was later managed by David Lees. (Cresswell returned to Coventry in 1985 and became manager of vehicle proving, on the retirement of the legendary Norman Dewis.)

Testing even took place in New York, where engineers drove 100 miles (160 km) each day over the tough city roads of Manhattan. By contrast, prototypes spent many months averaging 350 miles per day in the Australian outback, based at Cobar, New South Wales. Eighty-nine of the XJ40 prototypes were dedicated to durability-type running alone.

Retrospective
As a private company, Jaguar undertook stringent durability testing. After the opening of the MIRA proving ground at Lindley, near Nuneaton, in the early 1950s, the company also had a base where it could conduct tests of its competition models. Norman Dewis (who succeeded Ron Sutton in 1952), was chief of experimental vehicle testing for over thirty years, and was much involved in the early proving of the XJ40. Gaydon was also used by Jaguar when it was still a V-bomber base (later it was to become the headquarters of BL Technology). Overseas proving began seriously with the 1961 Mark Ten saloon, and this was stepped up throughout the 1960s and 1970s when hot and cold climate testing became essential for any serious exporter of high-class cars. Until the XJ40 project, however, there was never sufficient investment in prototypes or in test programmes, and the outstanding results achieved — especially in the original XJ6 — must be put down to good design and unremitting development: perfectionism is a Jaguar Engineering fetish.

ELECTRICAL SYSTEM
The XJ40 had to have the best and most advanced electrical system ever for a Jaguar. Many engineers in many countries helped to combine the elements of conventional systems (to avoid compromising the Jaguar's family personality) with electronics technology to create a reliable whole. The main

XJ40 total electrical system rig. The JDS unit can be seen in the background.

features are the use of a low-current earth line system incorporating fundamental changes in the design philosophy of the switches and connectors for ultra-reliable service. There is a central microprocessor unit plus others covering the instrumentation, air-conditioning, antilock braking, cruise control and engine management (one each for ignition and for fuelling). The system permits the use of much lighter harnesses, and all cables are resistant to climatic extremes.

ENGINES

The AJ6 aluminium engine family was first called the NJ6 (for 'New Jaguar'), but became the AJ6 (for 'Advanced Jaguar') in 1980. It has a complex background, and its links go back to the XK 6-cylinder and the V12 units. These links are due mainly to attempts at various times to amortize tooling costs by the sharing of manufacturing facilities — something that is not always possible when the time comes for quantity production. For example, the AJ6 shares the V12's bore-centre separation and, unnecessarily, the XK's main-bearing dimensions. The production Jaguar V12 has had a bore and stroke of 90 × 70 mm since it was introduced in 1971 in the Series Three E-type, and

Left *AJ6 3.6-litre dohc four-valve engine.*

Below *AJ6 2.9-litre sohc engine installed in the XJ40.*

in the XJ12 the following year. These dimensions were used on single-cylinder engine experiments in August 1970, featuring three-valve and four-valve configurations. Then, in July 1971, came the concept of a four-valve *production* V12; it was followed three months later by a 'slant-six' two-valve, still with a 'Sam Heron' cylinder head design featuring the flat face with a bowl in the piston. The last new '90 × 70' Jaguar engine idea seems to have been the 'Michael May' head design, drawn as a single-cylinder unit in February 1976 and in V12 form eight months later. Meanwhile, running on the bench (in 1973/74) there had been a heavily-ribbed four-valve alloy 3.6-litre 'half V12' measuring 92 × 90 mm. This was the beginning of the 'square' AJ6. Incidentally, it was Olaf von Fersen who first put Harry Mundy in touch with Michael May — already a pioneer of racing aerodynamics.

The relationship between the new product-planning section and Harry Mundy's Jaguar engine department was (in 1977) tenuous to say the least. One thing they had in common was a clear appreciation of the fact that, whatever might happen in the diesel field, a Jaguar-designed petrol unit must be allowed to prevail, in the face of a renewed Rover V8 threat. (There was also a feeling in many quarters that the fuel crisis would kill the V12 concept.)

It was in 1978 that Mundy introduced the 91/92 mm bore/stroke dimensions for the new six-cylinder engine — for the reason mentioned earlier (*see DIESEL ENGINE OPTION heading*). In 1979, the product planning submission for the NJ6 (AJ6) still indicated diesel, LPG, and four- and five-cylinder derivatives (for JRT use) as possibilities. The new six-cylinder engines were described as '2.9' and '3.8' litres.

However, it was the petrol-fuelled AJ6 (Advanced Jaguar Six, meaning six-cylinder form) which was to provide the final answer. If the V12 were to go, the four-valve AJ6 would replace it; when the 4.2 XK engine died, a two-valve version of the bigger AJ6 would be substituted; and the 3.4-litre XK engine would become obsolete when the 2.9-litre short-stroke high-compression AJ6 engine became available. However, the final announcement-day alternatives in 1986 were just a 3.6-litre four-valve (91 × 92 mm) and a 2.9-litre two-valve (91 × 74.8 mm). The two-valve 3.6 (formerly 3.8) was dropped, and the V12 would not fit. The latter situation was the sacrifice that Jaguar had had to make to ensure that it would not have to use other people's — i.e. Rover's — 'V' engines.

The twin-overhead-camshaft, four-valves-per-cylinder, 3.6-litre AJ6 engine was used first in the XJ-S, from autumn

1983, and in the XJ40 three years later. The two-valves-per-cylinder, 2.9-litre single-overhead-camshaft unit was introduced for the XJ40 only and for a limited number of markets.

Looking to the 1990s it seemed that there might be 3.2- and 4-litre versions of the twin-overhead-camshaft engine; and the revitalized V12 engine could offer more power without loss of economy.

The Jaguar V12 engine had become increasingly efficient, ever since petrol injection replaced carburettors and 'engine management' became increasingly frugal in the use of fuel, assisted by higher gearing. While the XJ40 structure was being engineered to take the V12, the engine itself was undergoing further development, and a 6.4-litre version was producing promising results. However, the very words 'six-point-four' *could* cause alarm in the market place, so it remained uncertain (when this book went to press) exactly what version of the V12 Jaguar would adopt to meet the BMW challenge of the 1990s.

Retrospective
In the 1930s, SS Cars fitted proprietary engines made by the Standard Motor Company. In 1935, William Lyons obtained permission to use a Weslake overhead-valve conversion, which put the new SS 'Jaguar' 2.7-litre models into the high-performance bracket. After the war Jaguar's all-new design arrived, the twin-overhead-camshaft XK engine; it was still being used for limousines and military vehicles long after the last Series Three XJ6 saloon had been built in the spring of 1987, and was expected to remain in production for a total of over forty years!

Back in the 1950s, Bill Heynes was instigating a project to make a V12 engine using two of the XK's twin-cam cylinder heads. Development of this idea was Harry Mundy's first job when he joined Jaguar from Autocar *in 1964. The road-going engine was tested in several Jaguar Mark Ten saloons; the racing version was used as a stressed member in the XJ13 mid-engined sports-racing prototype which might have taken Jaguar back into racing — but for the mergers that brought the company into British Leyland. (Incidentally, Heynes was also keen to put the 35/40 cylinder head into production.) The original four-overhead-camshaft V12 was bulky, heavy, complex, and did not prove an exceptional performer, although it did exceed 500 bhp on the bench in racing form. The present V12 block, as introduced in 1971, was designed as a pressure die casting — something else (like the four-cam engine) against which Harry Mundy fought hard.*

FUEL INJECTION
The 2.9-litre AJ6 engine has a Bosch LH Jetronic electronic fuel

injection system. The 3.6-litre unit's system, also electronically controlled, is by Lucas.

Retrospective
Jaguar chief power unit engineer, Trevor Crisp, first worked with fuel injection as an apprentice in the drawing office. The first fuel-injection XK engine to be photographed was fitted to a prototype Jaguar competition car which ran at a Le Mans practice session in the spring of 1954. That was an SU development, but Crisp's recollection is that the first serious Jaguar application was by Lucas. Certainly, it was a Lucas mechanical system which was raced successfully from 1956. (The last D-type to win Le Mans, in 1957, had Lucas fuel injection.) Tecalemit and Brico were other manufacturers with whom Crisp worked closely; for it had always been Jaguar's intention to adopt fuel injection — not because it offered better performance, necessarily, but because of the advantages of freedom on the induction side and automatic choke operation. Later, emission control legislation underlined the need for accuracy in engine fuelling, adding weight to the argument. The first use of fuel injection in series-production Jaguars was in 1975 for the V12 and 1978 for the 4.2-litre XK. However, twin SU carburettors remained standard wear for the XK-powered Daimler limousine which was still being produced at the rate of about five cars a week in 1987.

GEARBOX (MANUAL)

The XJ40's manual transmission is the Getrag 265 five-speed gearbox, already used by Jaguar in XJ-S 3.6 models. It is standard equipment on basic models, and a no-cost option on Sovereign and Daimler versions. A larger master cylinder gives the clutch on the saloon more disengagement travel than that on the XJ-S 3.6.

Retrospective
Jaguar's own gearboxes were not considered. The old four-speed synchromesh unit had been phased out in the early days of the XJ-S, and the very effective five-speed (advocated by Mundy) had been squashed during the 'England era' as being in insufficient demand to be worth manufacturing. This was no doubt true, but many people felt that there could have been a good market for it as a proprietary unit. The 'Rover Triumph' 77 mm five-speed gearbox was used on the Series Three XJ6, but was not 'man enough' to couple-up to the V12 engine. It was, however, specified for the XJ40 initially, and the 'Engineering Status' report of 1980/81 stated that 'other suppliers such as ZF have been approached but so far we have not found a satisfactory alternative'. The Getrag unit was, therefore, a fairly late candidate.

INTERIOR DESIGN

The first full XJ40 interior buck, or built-up model, in glass fibre was completed by the end of October 1980. The 'Engineering Status' report at the time declared that 'the response from all who have viewed the design has been most encouraging, the only criticisms being of the seat style' which (it was claimed) was not representative anyway, and would have changed before presentation to the BL board in February 1981.

Subsequent alterations resulted in a slightly more austere look than is normal for a Jaguar, and this was picked up at clinics in the USA and UK in 1983 when the Series Three's reputation had risen to such heights, and sales were so good, that the old model was becoming as much a yardstick for the new car as the usual German opposition. The model's austere look was soon replaced by traditional opulence in the XJ40. It did not necessarily make controls, switches and dials easy to design or locate, but the outcome was a compromise between traditional styling and modern information storage. At all levels of specification, the XJ40's interior is fully-equipped; of that — and of the ambience — there can be no doubt at all. The Loughborough Institute for Consumer Economics played a major role in the instrumentation.

The seating was designed following assessments on the Series Three by the Loughborough University Vehicle Ergonomics Group and the BL Technology advanced vehicle group at Gaydon. Final modifications were introduced as driver reports came in from Arizona, Canada, Australia and the UK,

The central console of the production model with manual transmission.

where hundreds of thousands of miles were being clocked-up in extreme conditions.

JDS (*See DIAGNOSTIC SYSTEM*)

J-GATE
This is the term given to the XJ40's unusual automatic transmission selector layout. It had started out as a 'U', rather than a 'J', in fact. This is an extract from the 1980/81 'Engineering Status' report: 'A new concept is proposed for this model, designed to...ensure that the criticisms levelled at our present gear change are overcome'. (A new layout was enforced by the inclusion of a fourth-speed position, anyway.) To increase the spacing between functions, the gate became a 'U' rather than a straight slot, in order to make it nigh-impossible for the driver inadvertently to engage neutral or reverse, and making manual over-ride selection a much more positive action. In due course, Jim Randle opted for the distinctive J-gate to achieve this objective.

LC40
This became the XJ40 project's designation for a while in BL circles. The 1977 'pre-concept' proposal prepared by Leyland Cars referred to 'LC40' but the project had become 'XJ40' again by May 1979 when product-planner Nigel Heslop presented his concept submission (for the AJ6 engine) to the JRT board. Most Jaguar-minded people kept on calling it 'XJ40' throughout; it was all part of the identity battle.

Layout for the automatic transmission control, or J-gate.

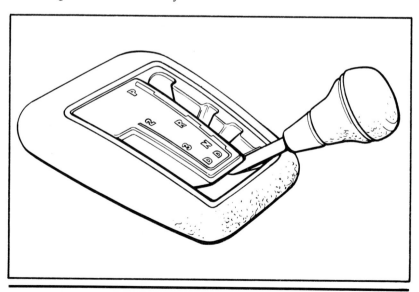

MANAGEMENT

Specific management of the XJ40 from a product engineering and development viewpoint was the responsibility of former Jaguar apprentice Malcolm Oliver. His task included the co-ordination of testing world-wide, to a degree never approached with the previous Jaguars. Early in 1987, Oliver was seconded to North America for a period covering the US launch of the new model.

NOISE AND VIBRATION

Suppression of these features had kept Jaguar ahead of the field for many years, and the XJ40 as introduced by Jim Randle and his team sustained this lead. To quote Randle in his 1986 Institution of Mechanical Engineers paper: 'Vibration should be at a barely discernible level...in simple terms XJ40 had to behave at least as well as the current vehicle, which is regarded by many as the best in the sector in this respect. How well that was achieved can be judged by the response characteristics illustrated...The test procedures used are unique to Jaguar, but are known accurate methods of judging refinement.'

PAINTWORK

As with several aspects of the XJ40 (notably the electronics), the paint finish had to meet completely new standards. Clear-over-base technology was new to Jaguar, and in fact the Coventry firm was the first motor manufacturer anywhere to use this technique for non-metallic as well as metallic-finish colours.

Interior noise comparisons between the Series Three XJ6 and its successor, the XJ40.

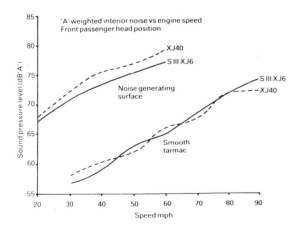

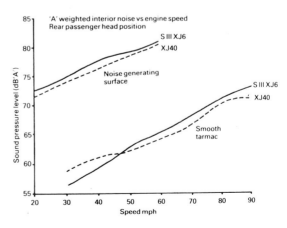

PRODUCT PLANNING

Such a term was unknown in the old Jaguar hierarchy. Later British Leyland systems were applied to Jaguar — not that Jaguar people necessarily took any notice, especially on the engineering side! Nevertheless, 'product planning' was probably of considerable help to them, however, when a pre-concept proposal of early 1977 stated that 'Business Plan volumes were compiled assuming that the V12 engine was retained as a "flagship" to the LC40 range'. However, it went on, 'Jaguar Product Planning consider that to make the 5.3 engine a design priority would compromise the size and weight and therefore the fuel consumption targets of all LC40 derivatives...On balance, we consider it most sensible that the LC40 is designed to meet the requirements of the volume-selling six-cylinder engines, and only afterwards should the feasibility of V12 fitment be considered.'

This plan was adhered to, but underlying it all was the ever-present danger (as Jaguar saw it) that the company would be forced into using a non-Jaguar petrol engine — ie, Rover's ex-GM V8. Consequently, Jaguar was quick to design the new car's structure so that, in its first form, XJ40 would not accept 'V' engines at all. Once the danger was past, there was still an element of risk in trying to market a V12 engine, but the pros outweighed the cons, and the XJ40 was well on the way to accepting the V12 as this book went to press.

Product Planning, run by Nigel Heslop, later provided the presentations for the big-investment submissions — for the AJ6 engine and the XJ40 itself which were to prove the keys to Jaguar's revival and the retention of its identity.

QUALITY

The highest product quality has always been paramount as a Jaguar ideal, but *not* always practical to achieve. Transformation of Jaguar's reputation for inconsistent quality to one of turning out regular excellence has been the work of everyone at Jaguar in recent years, and particularly of David Fielden, quality director, and his team. A full technical audit proposal was prepared for Randle's 'Engineering Status' report by BL Technology director Charles Maple, who had introduced military-style systems into BL car quality assessment during the 1970s. In his introduction, he stressed the quality achieved by Mercedes-Benz and BMW compared with that of the 1980 Jaguar Series Three. 'The new model,' he wrote, 'must achieve an enormous improvement in quality and reliability to meet the standards set by its competitors, and the XJ40 warranty

XJ40 on rig test.

objectives represent a considerable challenge to all involved in its design and manufacture.' XJ40 product development manager Malcolm Oliver was the linchpin of the programme to design quality into the car from the very start; while Derek Waelend was the man responsible for translating the XJ40 into a series-production reality.

RIG-TEST PROGRAMME
Apart from the durability running of complete cars, Jaguar carried out a comprehensive programme of component rig testing. For the XJ40, the programme required the design and construction of a large number of dedicated rigs, and even the establishment of a separate rig design and manufacturing department.

Among the ninety-four special rigs constructed at Jaguar was a 'four-poster' electro-hydraulic rig to simulate the vibrations and stresses of road and proving ground surfaces. Jaguar's in-house rig-test programme was supplemented by equivalent ones at suppliers, where 384 different rigs were constructed to test components.

In his 1980/81 'Engineering Status' report, Randle had emphasized the importance of 'a considerable increase' in rig-test facilities, and a new building was quickly commissioned to accommodate this and other important development activity with minimal disruption of work in the engineering department.

SERVICING
A return to the principle of specialist servicing had already done

Opposite *This specification was issued for the UK announcement on 8 October 1986. (The XJ40 would not be introduced into the US market until the summer of 1987, as the 1988 model XJ6 and Vanden Plas sedans.) Prices in UK varied between £16,500 for the 'manual' 2.9 and £28,500 for the Daimler.*

wonders for the marque's image by the time the XJ40 was announced.

From the initial concept, Jaguar service engineers were involved in the new car's design to keep routine maintenance bills down and reduce the costs of repairs and component replacement. As a result service intervals for the new range, at 7,500 miles (12,000 km) and 15,000 miles (24,000 km), are less frequent than for competitive luxury saloons. Over 50,000 miles (80,000 km), the XJ40 incurs only fourteen hours of labour charges. On similar luxury saloons the equivalent figure can be as high as twenty hours for routine maintenance.

All the components were, therefore, designed from the outset to be more easily repaired or replaced. For example the time needed to replace a fuel tank on an XJ6 3.6 is 1.8 hours — virtually half the 3.3 hours needed on the Series Three. The reduction in man-hours to replace all four brake discs has been dramatically reduced to a little over two hours — compared with nine hours on the Series Three saloons. Similarly, to replace the electric motor on the sliding sunroof should take some twenty minutes compared with forty-eight minutes previously.

A new diagnostic system (*see separate heading*), or JDS, is described by Jaguar as 'the most advanced fault-diagnosing system ever presented by a major manufacturer to its dealer network'. It was developed for use in all markets and is giving dealers a powerful tool for customer support. Simply by plugging into JDS a technician can identify a problem on any one of the seven principal electrical or electronic systems on the vehicle and quickly resolve the fault.

There are now fewer service outlets than before but they are more committed. Indeed, a number of long-established dealerships have been retained for their loyalty, efficiency and dedication through thick and thin. What was evident by 1987 was that a new breed of Jaguar dealer had emerged — responding, like the customer, to new and improved products, and to the motivation behind them. With the XJ40, it could be said for the first time, hand-on-heart, that a Jaguar had been engineered with servicing in mind.

SPECIFICATION

The first published specification of a new model is always an important document, yet in later years it can be difficult to find. No book can be completely comprehensive in its scope. In this one, though, I have tried to identify some XJ40 landmarks, within the context of Jaguar history, and so the original UK specification is published on an adjacent page. The major

	XJ6 2·9	XJ6 3·6	Sovereign 2·9	Sovereign 3·6	Daimler 3·6
ENGINE TYPE	AJ6 in line 6 cyl.	AJ6 in line 6 cyl.	AJ6 in line 6 cyl.	AJ6 in line 6 cyl.	AJ6 in line 6 cyl.
	aluminium alloy	aluminium alloy	aluminium alloy	aluminium alloy	aluminium alloy
	head/block SOHC	head/block DOHC	head/block SOHC	head/block DOHC	head/block DOHC
	2 valves/cyl.	4 valves/cyl.	2 valves/cyl.	4 valves/cyl.	4 valves/cyl.
Displacement (cm³)	2919	3590	2919	3590	3590
Bore × Stroke (mm)	91 × 74.8	91 × 92	91 × 74.8	91 × 92	91 × 92
Compression ratio	12.6:1	9.6:1	12.6:1	9.6:1	9.6:1
Max. power DIN BHP (kW) @ rev/min	165 (123) @ 5000	221 (165) @ 5000	165 (123) @ 5600	221 (165) @ 5000	221 (165) @ 5000
Max. torque DIN lb/ft (Nm) @ rev/min	176 (239) @ 4000	248 (337) @ 4000	176 (239) @ 4000	248 (337) @ 4000	248 (337) @ 4000
Combustion chambers	May high efficiency	Pent root	May high efficiency	Pent root	Pent root
Ignition system	Bosch electronic	Lucas electronic	Bosch electronic	Lucas electronic	Lucas electronic
Fuel system	Bosch electronic injection	Lucas electronic injection	Bosch electronic injection	Lucas electronic injection	Lucas electronic injection
TRANSMISSION TYPE	Getrag 5 speed manual	Getrag 5 speed manual	ZF 4 speed automatic	ZF 4 speed automatic	ZF 4 speed automatic
Top gear ratio (5th man/4th auto)	0.76:1	0.76:1	0.73:1	0.73:1	0.73:1
Final drive ratio	3.77:1	3.54:1	4.09:1	3.54:1	3.54:1
MPH/1000 rev/min (5th man/4th auto)	26.6	28.3	24.5	29.5	29.5
WHEEL TYPE/SIZE	Steel 390 × 180mm to 35	Steel 390 × 180mm to 35	Steel 390 × 180mm to 35	Steel 390 × 180mm to 35	Alloy 390 × 180mm to 35
Tyre size	220/65 VR 390 TD	220/65 VR 390 TD	220/65 VR 390 TD	220/65 VR 390 TD	220/65 VR 390 TD
DRAG COEFFICIENT	0.37	0.37	0.37	0.37	0.37
BRAKING SYSTEM	Hydraulic power boost assisted 4 wheel disc brakes ventilated at front. Safety split front and rear circuits with fluid level, pad wear and low boost pressure warning. Hand operated mechanical parking brake on rear wheels.		Hydraulic power boost assisted 4 wheel disc brakes ventilated at front. Bosch 4 wheel sensing anti-lock braking system with yaw control. Safety split front and rear circuits with fluid level, pad wear, low boost pressure and anti lock failure warning. Hand operated mechanical parking brake on rear wheels.		
STEERING	Rack and pinion power assisted steering with 2.8 turns lock to lock. Collapsible steering column with axial adjustment. Turning circle 40ft 8in. (12.4m) between kerbs.				
SUSPENSION FRONT	Fully independent with unequal length upper and lower wishbones arranged to provide anti-dive effect under braking. Steel coil springs, telescopic dampers and anti-roll bar.				
REAR	Fully independent with hubs located at lower ends by wishbones and driveshafts acting as upper links. Wishbones designed for anti squat and anti-lift under acceleration and braking.				
	Concentric steel coil springs and dampers.		Concentric steel coil springs and hydraulic ride levelling struts.		
BODY CONSTRUCTION	4 door saloon. All steel monocoque construction with front and rear crumple zones including front crush tubes. Impact absorbing wrap around bumpers. One piece bodyside.				
PAINT AND PROTECTION	Box sections and closed members hot wax injected. Zinc coated undertrame panels. Cathodic electro-coat. Clear over base paint process with automated electrostatic application of primer/sealer and clear coats. Twin colour coats.				
PERFORMANCE					
Acceleration 0-60 m.p.h. (s)	9.6	7.4	10.8	8.8	8.8
Top speed m.p.h. (km/h)	120 (193)	136 (219)	118 (190)	135 (217)	135 (217)
ECONOMY					
Urban cycle m.p.g. (l/100 km)	19.5 (14.5)	18.6 (15.2)	19.8 (14.3)	18.7 (15.1)	18.7 (15.1)
56 m.p.h. – m.p.g. (l/100 km)	38.7 (7.3)	35.8 (7.9)	36.2 (7.8)	36.2 (7.8)	36.2 (7.8)
75 m.p.h. – m.p.g. (l/100 km)	31.0 (9.1)	29.7 (9.5)	27.4 (10.3)	30.4 (9.3)	30.4 (9.3)
WEIGHT					
Max kerb weight lb (kg) with options	3793 (1720)	3903 (1770)	3793 (1720)	3903 (1770)	3903 (1770)
Gross weight lb (kg) max permissible	4719 (2140)	4829 (2190)	4719 (2140)	4829 (2190)	4829 (2190)

Dimensions	XJ6	Sovereign	Daimler

Note: Dimensions will vary from car to car due to design and production tolerances, the nominal condition has been used wherever possible.

		XJ6	Sovereign	Daimler
A	Overall length in (mm)	196.4 (4988)	196.4 (4988)	196.4 (4988)
B	Overall width incl. mirrors in (mm)	78.9 (2005)	78.9 (2005)	78.9 (2005)
C	Overall height in (mm)	54.3 (1380)	53.5 (1358)	53.5 (1358)
D	Ground clearance – min at GVW in (mm)	4.7 (120)	5.1 (130)	5.1 (130)
E	Track width – front in (mm)	59.1 (1500)	59.1 (1500)	59.1 (1500)
F	Track width – rear in (mm)	59.0 (1498)	59.0 (1498)	59.0 (1498)
G	Wheelbase in (mm)	113.0 (2870)	113.0 (2870)	113.0 (2870)
H	Max. legroom – driver in (mm)	41.1 (1045)	41.1 (1045)	41.1 (1045)
I	Max. legroom – front pass. in (mm)	45.1 (1145)	45.1 (1145)	42.4* (1077)*
J	Min. legroom – rear outboard in (mm)	34.0 (863)	33.1 (843)	33.1* (843)*
K	Max. headroom – front in (mm)	38.7 (983)	38.7 (983)	36.6 (930)
L	Max. headroom – rear in (mm)	36.5 (928)	36.5 (928)	36.8 (935)
M	Shoulder width – front in (mm)	57.5 (1460)	57.5 (1460)	57.5 (1460)
N	Shoulder width – rear in (mm)	57.6 (1463)	57.6 (1463)	57.6 (1463)
O	Boot volume cu ft (mm³)	15.1 (0.43)	15.1 (0.43)	15.1 (0.43)
P	Fuel tank capacity Imp. gal. (litres)	19.5 (88.6)	19.5 (88.6)	19.5 (88.6)

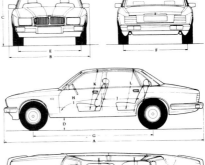

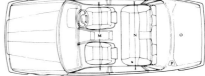

* With passenger footwell rugs fitted

differences for other significant markets are related to national exhaust emission control regulations.

SUSPENSION (FRONT)

The independent front suspension is similar to that on previous XJ models, although all the components are new. Characteristic features include transverse wishbones top and bottom, while anti-drive geometry has been retained. A noteworthy item, specified early on, is the containment of bump and rebound control within the (Boge) dampers, thus reducing bending loads on the wishbones, and also saving weight.

Retrospective
The company's first development engineer, Walter Hassan, began working on independent front suspension soon after joining the company in 1938, under chief engineer William Heynes. Both admired the Citroën traction avant's torsion bar independent front suspension (IFS), although a number of different schemes were tried. The definitive Jaguar IFS — top and bottom wishbones, longitudinal torsion

Although similar to that of previous XJ models, the front suspension of the XJ40 was new, with no 'carry-over' components.

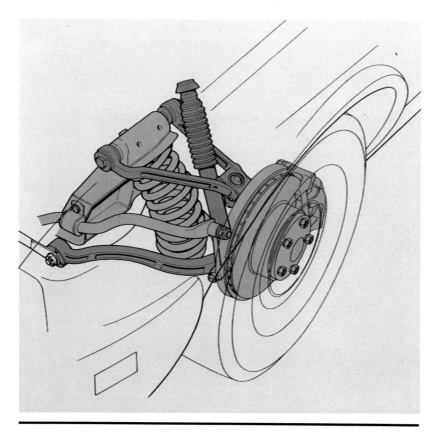

bars, and telescopic shock absorbers — was announced in September 1948, as part of the Mark Five's specification. The fitting of IFS to a subframe was seen seven years later on the 2.4 saloon which featured coil spring units, partly because it would be difficult to mount torsion bars in the monocoque. The noise-insulating subframe has been a Jaguar feature ever since.

SUSPENSION (REAR)

The rear suspension of the XJ40 is (to quote the 1980/81 'Engineering Status' report) 'a unique design incorporating quite substantial compliance and involving the use of a pendular link at the front end of the wishbone and a duplex mounted beam at the rear. The links are devised in such a way as to place all the loads at the front mounting bushes so that weight transfer and torque effects are in opposition, reducing wind-up and allowing much lower-stiffness mountings than would be otherwise possible, thus reducing the transmission of axle and road noise.' This complex yet logical design typifies the

The production version of the 'compliant' system, which provided an improved combination of shock isolation, noise suppression and road behaviour.

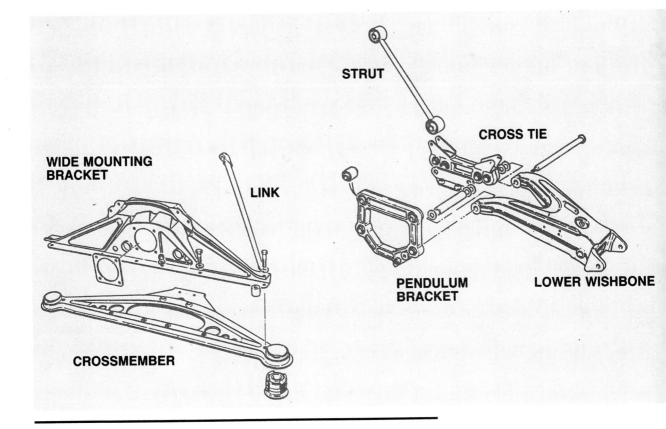

WIDE MOUNTING BRACKET

LINK

STRUT

CROSS TIE

PENDULUM BRACKET

LOWER WISHBONE

CROSSMEMBER

One of several shelved rear suspension developments was this one, incorporating two-speed final drive which had been a serious project at one stage.

Rear suspension on test: the principles if not the materials are well-established.

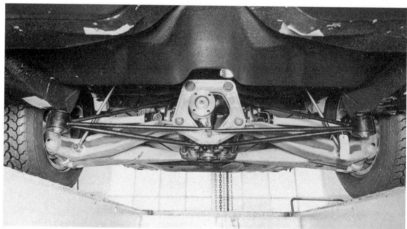

work of the director of product engineering, Jim Randle, who is dedicated to maintaining Jaguar's perfectionist aims. Its effectiveness has become familiar to all who have driven the XJ40. (Rear ride-levelling is standard or available throughout the XJ40 range.)

Retrospective

Several all-independently sprung military prototypes were designed during the early 1940s, but they appear to have had no direct bearing on civilian vehicle design. Fully-independent suspension was tried experimentally on the D-type competition car in the mid-1950s, and adopted for its road-going E-type derivative, introduced in early 1961. The latter's design was carried on through all subsequent sports and saloon car ranges, starting with the Mark Ten (autumn 1961). The original XJ6 was to have had a new independent rear suspension (IRS) system which reflected Bob Knight's aim to achieve what has been achieved in the XJ40 — compliance without adverse effect on steering. Tom Jones (David Tree's predecessor on vehicle design) recalls that he worked with Knight on a torque-tube system that did away with a subframe, with dampers mounted direct to the body structure. They kept running into problems with tracking and with an unacceptable booming; the tracking fault was traced to the front suspension and eliminated, but, to quote Jones, 'that boom ''spoofed'' us...We were running out of time, and went back to a layout based on the existing IRS'. Lyons had told Heynes, and Heynes had told Knight, that no more time must be wasted; and so that system was discarded. This fact resulted in the original XJ's rear body structure looking as though it had not been designed to take the rear suspension subframe. Indeed it wasn't!

By the time the first XJ6 was announced in 1968, Jim Randle was well established on the research side, and he went on to make suspension design a speciality. Although there are elements of stillborn designs to be found in the XJ40's rear suspension, the final concept involving the 'pendulum' is down to Randle. Many other rear ends had been tried in the interim, including a serious two-speed axle exercise which was eventually dropped, like so many other experiments that could not live up to Jaguar's standards of refinement in operation.

TYRES

Perhaps the most important aspect of the tyres is the bead-locking safety feature, first specified as 'Denloc' (1980/81 'Engineering Status') but, subsequently, presented as a joint development — the Dunlop-Michelin TD. The TD wheel rim has a special groove in which the TD trapezoidal tyre's beading is locked, reducing the adverse effect of sudden deflation (as proved most effectively by Jaguar's official TWR racing team, which used bead-locking tyres from 1984).

Retrospective
Jaguar and Dunlop worked closely on tyre development — especially from 1950, when the first serious racing programme began.

U-GATE (*see J-GATE*)

VALUE

Price and value-for-money had been key factors in the company's early days. Jaguar's clever initial marketing policy made sure that the XJ40 carried on the tradition. The cheapest version to be introduced on the home market in October 1986 was a 2.9-litre manual transmission XJ6 at £16,495, while the top model in the XJ40 range was the 3.6-litre Daimler, selling at

£28,495. Even at this price the 3.6 was nearly £500 cheaper than a BMW 635CSi and £1,200 less than the Mercedes-Benz 420SEL. At the other end of the range the 'basic' (yet fully equipped) Jaguar was undercutting the Rover Sterling and Ford Scorpio 'executive' cars — *and* the cheapest Porsches, too. However, the need to offer value for money was not allowed to compromise the quest for engineering excellence.

'V' ENGINES

Initially, the XJ40 was offered only with a straight-six, but it was being adapted to take the V12 engine for the 1990s. This delay can be put down to Jaguar's instinct for self-preservation (see below).

Retrospective

A Jaguar 60-degree V8 was tested in the late 1960s, and found to have an uneven beat which could not be eliminated completely. There were too many V8 engines in BL already (Daimler, Rover, and Triumph) and in the 1970s, after the other three had been shelved, there were strenuous efforts to get Jaguar to fit the (ex-GM) Rover unit. Even more strenuous efforts at Browns Lane prevented this happening but, by making the V8's fitment into XJ40 impossible, Jaguar's engineers also ruled out the use of their own V12. At the time it looked doomed, on the grounds of its fuel consumption and the related OPEC crisis. Then changed circumstances meant that a V12-engined XJ40 would be made in due course, after all.

WHEELS

These were given specially designed tyre-bead gripping grooves to reduce the effect of punctures upon car control, and to allow the driver time to find a safe stopping place. (Four-wheel drive is, not unnaturally, on the menu for the 1990s.)

'XJ' NUMBERS

The internal numbering system is complex and inconsistent. It began just before the war, according to retired chassis engineer Tom Jones. He thinks 'X' meant 'experimental', that XA was a Jaguar chassis project, and XB a military one. It is recorded in a technical paper by Bill Heynes that XF, XG, XJ and XK were engine designations, the last being adopted for the production engine and the sports-car range itself. So it may be that all the early 'X' designations referred to engines.

'XJ' terminology started after the war and, apparently, was replaced by 'EXP' numbers for a time. The first 'modern' XJ project seems to be 'XJ3' (known to the Pressed Steel Co as

'Utah', and to the customer as the 3.4- and 3.8-litre S-type saloon, introduced in 1963). 'XJ4' was the project which led to the XJ6 of 1968; 'XJ5' was a major structural change to the Mark Ten (or 'Zenith') for air flow/air-conditioning; 'XJ6' was the four-overhead-camshaft V12 racing engine, 'XJ8' was the first 2+2 version of the E-type coupé…and so on. The only one (prior to 'XJ40') to become known by its codename *outside* the works was, of course, the 'XJ13' mid-engined sports-racing prototype. The system has not been used in an orderly way, however, as there appear to have been subsequent duplications and omissions, so a comprehensive list of XJ numbers and their subjects would be hard to compile on present information.

Meanwhile, to add to the list, the Jaguar 420 of 1966 carried the code number 'XJ16', the Series Two E-types were 'XJ22' and 'XJ23', while the original XJ-S was 'XJ27'. 'XJ50' is the Series Three V12 saloon, and the 3.6-litre XJ-Ss are 'XJ57' and 'XJ58'.

XJ40

The 'XJ40' project number covers the new range of XJ6, Sovereign, and Daimler six-cylinder 2.9- and 3.6-litre saloon cars announced on 8 October 1986. Since the names of the cars have not been altered (from Series Three), and since a 'Series Four' designation is being eschewed at all costs, XJ40 is likely to remain useful terminology for instant identification. Future models will probably maintain the XJ internal numbering code in some form. 'XJ41' has been used already (for the 3.4-litre XK-engined XJ6 saloon which was developed to replace the unsatisfactory 2.8), yet it is also in use for a future sporting derivative — and has been for many years (BL's product planners called it 'LC41'). One day I hope to resolve the whole XJ numbering problem! I should add that the Daimler name is not used in the USA, where the top-of-the-range XJ40 is being called the 'Jaguar Vanden Plas'.

5

BUILDING IN THE QUALITY

Jaguar styling and engineering have an exemplary record, comparable with that of Mercedes-Benz, BMW, and Porsche. However, the same cannot be said of Jaguar manufacturing facilities; or, at least, not until the mid-1980s.

With an operation the scale of Jaguar's, only a continuous build-up of production and profit could lead to major investment in modern computer-aided manufacturing technology. The XJ40 investment — some £200 million of it — was the springboard for the biggest single leap forward the company had taken in its entire history. This investment was intended to help provide for future versions of the XJ40, plus new sports and personal luxury cars, and to cater for an increase in manufacturing capacity of ten to fifteen per cent a year. Sir John Egan was determined to maintain the momentum throughout his organization, both by example and by delegation. He was not going to run before he could walk (as Geoffrey Robinson had done in 1974), nor was he going to be too frugal in financing the future (as Jaguar's founder, Sir William Lyons, had undoubtedly been). Yet, within five years of Egan's arrival, the company was surpassing its previous production and profit records, and the upward trend was still strong in mid 1987, despite international currency fluctuations.

Before describing the new approach to manufacturing Jaguar cars, a little background will highlight the company's progress in this area.

Traditional craftsmanship-based skills were used in the days of Swallow bodies and SS cars. On two occasions — in 1929 and 1938 — the company nearly folded due to attempts at shortcutting body-making procedures. Lyons later bought a neighbouring manufacturer (Motor Panels) but sold it again for reasons best known to himself. It may have been that he wanted to release cash for the post-war re-start of car production (which included the first in-house engine manufacture) or was having labour problems. Either way, Jaguar had to rely on the Pressed Steel Company and other smaller firms from then on. Such reliance on outsiders went against the grain, and Lyons and his general manager (and deputy chairman) Arthur Whittaker never overcame the problem entirely.

Engine manufacture was undertaken to high standards on generally old machines, and by the 1960s only minimal automation had been introduced; my recollection is that the first transfer machine was a Renault item for the XK crankshaft line. In 1969–70 a new £3 million V12 engine production line was installed at the Radford, Coventry, works, and this was the most costly simple manufacturing project undertaken by the old company. Lyon's investment had been in expansion, rather than in modernization of equipment.

The move from Swallow Road to the former Daimler No2 shadow factory at Browns Lane (about two miles away) was carried out brilliantly, thanks to a dedicated staff — notably production director John Silver and purchase manager Harry Teather — who saw to it that the workers accompanied their machines to the new site and had the material to start work again as soon as the equipment was properly installed and plugged into the mains. Despite the disruption of the move, production increased over this period.

Another example of Jaguar teamwork at its best occurred in February 1957, after a fire destroyed about one third of the main factory building at its northern end. Employees and suppliers saw to it that the production lines were back in action very quickly, and another record year of production ensued.

Those were inspiring times, with regular victories at Le Mans and elsewhere to keep the Jaguar name in the news, and advanced new model ranges (the E-type and Mark Ten) in preparation. But there was not enough plant modernization. Exhortations to produce top quality goods hung above the work areas, yet also pride was taken in the frequency of inspection of components at almost every stage of a Jaguar's manufacture and assembly. It seemed the right thing at the time, but it does not seem so now.

Through the 1960s, car production settled at a fairly constant 25,000 cars a year, but the business was enlarged by diversification into commerical vehicles and industrial equipment with the purchase of Daimler (1960), Guy (1961), Coventry Climax (1963), and Meadows (1964). Luxury saloons and sports cars were supplemented almost throughout the decade by the compact Mark Two (and/or derivations from it) plus, for a time, the last all-Daimler designs — the Majestic Major and the SP250 — which had 90-degree V8 engines of proved performance. These Daimler 2.5-litre and 4.5-litre power units were taken out of the manufacturing system by 1970, however, on the grounds that complete re-tooling would have been necessary to achieve Jaguar volumes. This was undoubtedly true — but so was the fact that they had not been designed in the Jaguar engineering department which was, at about the same time, discarding its own unsatisfactory 60-degree V8. So, far from being superseded (as intended), the grand old XK straight-six was to soldier on through the 1970s and 1980s, accompanied by the new 60-degree V12.

By the early 1970s, the Jaguar Group had lost control of Coventry Climax and Guy Motors to other areas of BL; sadly, Daimler bus manufacture was transferred to Leyland, Lancs, where it died a quiet death.

The Daimler works at Radford, Coventry, had become Jaguar's manufacturing plant shortly after the 1960 purchase. The machine shops and related functions had been moved the three miles from Browns Lane, which could then be laid out more effectively as an assembly plant.

What was needed, above all, was a modern paint facility. A new installation by Carrier Engineering, soon after the fire, was known as 'Number Two Paintshop'; it was in effect a 'final coat' shop, utilized after road-testing and mechanical 'sign-off', and

Transformed many times since it was bought (as 'The Daimler') by Jaguar in 1960, the Radford works now possesses multi-million-pound manufacturing equipment of the latest kind, as exemplified by this transfer line — part of the £30m AJ6 engine investment programme.

the work involved the mammoth task of masking brightwork, glass, and wheel apertures. In theory, this second paintshop minimized the effects of inadvertent damage; in practice, this led to a great deal of overspray — and sometimes it showed.

One of Geoffrey Robinson's first actions in his short but meteoric tenure as the BL-appointed head of Jaguar was to announce a scheduled doubling of production within two years. This plan was put into action very quickly and an Italian company called Interlack won the tender to install a new paint plant. The structural material arrived at Browns Lane...and just sat there, waiting. It lay there through the winter of the Ryder investigation (1974–75) and for several winters after that.

The brief period (1978–79) known as 'Jaguar Rover Triumph II' put Jaguar manufacturing at greatest risk, however, with strong arguments for putting Jaguar assembly into Solihull (the under-utilized new Rover plant) and the possible closure of either Radford or Browns Lane — or both. Instead of building a new paintshop at Browns Lane, it was decided to paint Jaguars at the Castle Bromwich, Birmingham, plant originally commissioned as a Nuffield shadow factory for the manufacture of Supermarine Spitfire fighters in April 1938. In early 1979, however, Mike Beasley was having to organize the revival of facilities at Browns Lane, because bodies coming from Castle Bromwich in the then-new thermo-plastic acrylic finish were having to be repainted completely in Coventry. In December 1979, the situation was still bad, and Bob Knight obtained 'unanimous' support for his proposal to acquire, at an estimated £8 million, paint facilities from the Triumph plant at Speke, Liverpool which, in theory, could come on stream in 1982. (At that same meeting, both Knight and Beasley welcomed the thought of eliminating the damage often caused in transit between Castle Bromwich and Browns Lane, while David Fielden made it clear that the paint issue must not be used to excuse other quality problems which were being put in hand.)

The 'Speke plan' came to nothing, however, and Beasley and his colleagues were faced with bigger problems than ever as Castle Bromwich seized up and 'Jaguar Rover Triumph II' proved impracticable.

There were two important meetings with Michael Edwardes and these reinforced his conviction that, despite its difficulties in launching the Series Three satisfactorily, and an alarming drop in demand for the XJ-S, Jaguar *should* be allowed to find a way of going it alone. The crunch point came in 1980, when BL indicated its intention to close down Castle Bromwich, proposing that it would take Jaguar bodies from its Swindon plant to Cowley for painting before onward transit to Browns Lane. This was just too much.

The conflict was brewing when John Egan arrived, and on 10 June 1980 national and Midland daily newspapers carried a story of great significance: that of a change of Castle Bromwich management. Arthur Smith told *Financial Times* readers: 'BL moved quickly yesterday to deny suggestions that transfer of control of Castle Bromwich marked the first move towards selling Jaguar as a separate operation. The company stressed Jaguar was crucial to BL's model range and there was no intention to allow a sale.'

Birmingham Post readers that day got a different angle from Jane Pickard who had been talking to Jaguar's founder and honorary president: 'News that Jaguar is to control its own body shell manufacture restores once more the prospect of the prestige company controlling its own destiny. Like the cat which walked by itself, Jaguar has never found it easy to hunt as a pack animal. The embrace of BL has been suffocating...Sir William Lyons is retired but acts as a consultant at Jaguars. He believes that the company has to regain its independence to become successful again. Although he presided over the mergers which swamped the once-autonomous company, Sir William points to the final move into BL as the point when the problems started: "The mergers worked out badly when BMC amalgamated with Leyland. The point was that Leyland came in and more-or-less took over BMC. The problems today come from then, but I hope now to see an end to them." '

Jane Pickard went on to comment on the long-running dispute over the siting of the new paint shop, and reported that a car-sticker campaign (by the unions, urging autonomy) was blowing up into a 'full-scale war of independence'. The workers had been furious over the decision to move 'their' paint shop away from Browns Lane, and were gleefully crowing 'I told you so' when Castle Bromwich ran into trouble.

Taking over Castle Bromwich and obtaining union acceptance of the situation were vitally important. Mike Beasley and transport union convenor David Holloway had established a form of harmony during the long and bitter battle. Employee relations manager Harry Adey, himself a former union man, recalls Holloway as a leading moderate at a time of great militancy.

David Holloway suffered a stroke shortly after John Egan's arrival at Browns Lane and could not return to participate in the exciting new era. These were the words Holloway left for the

Birmingham Post to quote: 'We are told there is a high demand for Jaguars...Egan's frankness has impressed me, and he has asked for an opportunity to prove himself.' John Egan delivered the goods — but six years were to pass before a totally satisfactory paint process could be installed. For the time being, Jaguar overhauled the existing TPA system to bring quality up to a satisfactory level, while plans were laid to bridge the gap to what is openly called 'Mercedes quality'. But it had to take time — not just for technological reasons but because Jaguar would have to fund its own future once it was on the road to independence. (It should be noted that, before 1984's privatization, Jaguar repaid close on £100 million to BL, thereby helping to fund the Austin Rover Group.)

However, not *every* plan to update Jaguar's manufacturing technology was right first time; but the occasional hiccup was only to be expected in what amounted to a mammoth operation to give Jaguar the modernization it had needed so desperately and for so long.

Each aspect of Jaguar's revival could fill a book on its own, so we must restrict ourselves to picking out the highlights.

To me, the main feature of the manufacturing story is the combination of team spirit and professionalism that the Egan philosophy has brought about. As in vehicle engineering, there is in this area of Jaguar a mixture of long-term experience and new blood. Central to the manufacturing organization is Mike Beasley, whose appointment to the post of assistant managing director in January 1986 was a measure of Egan's faith in him and of their success in recruiting the right people to bring in new methods while introducing the XJ40.

Michael Ernest Beasley (born 18 July 1943) was educated in his home town, Slough, where he undertook an apprenticeship with Satchwell Controls and achieved high qualifications in mechanical and production engineering. Between the ages of twenty-two and thirty he gained experience in process engineering with the Ford Motor Company. He was with Jaguar briefly in 1974 before joining Leyland Cars as plant and equipment engineering manager on the body and assembly side. In 1977, following the sudden death of Peter Craig, he was appointed plant director at Browns Lane, becoming manu-facturing director of Jaguar Cars as the marque's identity began to re-emerge, and control of the Radford plant was regained.

Ford's thinking has little in common with Jaguar's in terms of product engineering or styling, as the personnel records could prove. The same records could also show that Ford has been able to supply Jaguar with just the men it needed to fulfil

Michael Beasley, assistant managing director (centre) *with* (left to right): *Walter Turner, director of Browns Lane plant; Patrick Audrain, director, purchasing; Brian Savage, director manufacturing engineering; David Fielden, director, quality; Gerard Lawlor, director of Castle Bromwich plant; Eynon Thomas, director of Radford plant; Jim Macaffer, director, material control; and Derek Waelend, director, manufacture, who was to leave Jaguar for Lotus in May 1987.*

Right and opposite top *Diagram and detail view of Comau body-side automation installed at Castle Bromwich, Birmingham, and fully operational during 1987.*

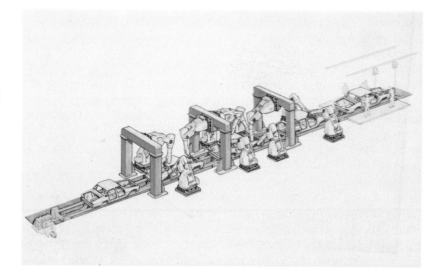

manufacturing functions which had never existed before. The 'work hard, play hard' men of the mid-1970s had not lasted long enough to prove themselves: the later wave from Ford was to show itself to be in a completely different category.

When the XJ40 was approaching the pilot-build stage, the need for a project director became evident. Derek Waelend (born 23 March 1944) was finding himself 'boxed off' at Ford, due to the fact that American and German executives tend to get priority in Ford's management structure. This was

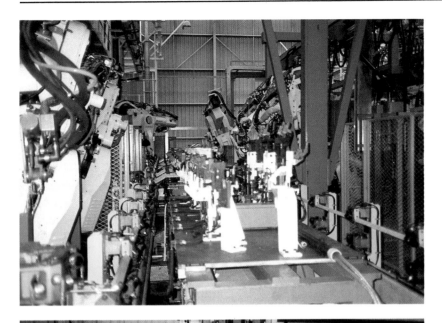

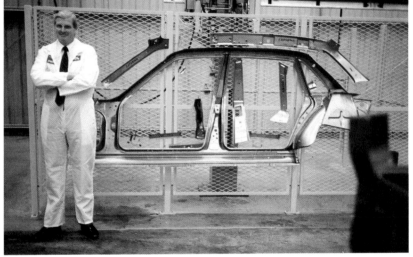

Plant director Gerry Lawlor with an example of the mono-side — one item of many in a vast programme which is bringing Jaguar manufacturing technology right up to date.

especially disillusioning for Waelend, who had accomplished great things ever since his early days as an apprentice toolmaker and the start of his arduous climb up the body production ladder. He takes pride in his involvement in setting up Fiesta production in Spain and the highly automated Escort body plant at Halewood.

At a time that the opportunity to move to Jaguar presented itself, Waelend was thinking of joining Land-Rover. But he opted for Jaguar in June 1983, appreciating the way in which

Egan delegated authority, as this would create an ideal chance for dealing with resistance to change. Waelend's quicksilver temperament and dynamism helped to put Jaguar's launch target into a proper perspective. When he arrived, there was still talk of launching the XJ40 in 1984. 'Del-boy' Waelend made clear what was probably only slightly short of obvious: if the job was to be done properly, the car could not be announced until 1986. This also helped Egan to come to his decision about the timing of privatization.

Waelend put the pilot-build facility on course for consistent production and it became operational in 1984. Soon Waelend was made director of manufacturing while Beasley moved up into the new post of assistant managing director. Suddenly, however, in May 1987 Waelend left Jaguar and joined Lotus after barely four years in Coventry.

There was other Ford recruitment, and the most important new appointment was that of another go-getter, Brian Savage (born 16 July 1939), whose speciality was paint. He had been with Ford for almost twenty years when Waelend put the wheels in motion for bringing him into the Jaguar team. Savage was faced with a difficult decision, as he had recently been promoted after a period of secondment to Ford Köln. However, he made the move and, as staff director of manufacturing engineering, Savage set about completing the first major Jaguar plant modernization plan.

Earlier plans for collaboration with the Preston-based Anglo-Japanese company Dainichi Sykes fell by the wayside and an altogether more ambitious programme was embarked upon with the Italian giant, Comau, for £36 million worth of automated body-in-white robot welding equipment. The preliminary phase — a £2.7 million body-side manufacturing cell — was installed in 'C' Block, Castle Bromwich, during 1986, at about the same time as the long-awaited clear-over-base paint shop came on stream.

It was expected that, when the Comau equipment was fully operational, it would be one of the most advanced installations of its kind — and to some extent unique, because of its capability for switching to different bodies with minimal loss of production. Moreover, it could be relied upon to reproduce accurately, and consistently, to specification.

To many people, not least to plant director Gerry Lawlor and paint shop manager David Hudson (later to move to Browns Lane) Castle Bromwich has been a revelation, providing space for new techniques without interruption of current production. Whatever anyone may have felt in the dark days, the 'gift' of

Castle Bromwich represents a miracle which could not have happened at Browns Lane without the sacrifice of some other essential facility. As for the safe transportation of painted bodies from Birmingham to Coventry — once a source of worry — this is now taken for granted.

The rebirth of Castle Bromwich has also brought Browns Lane and Radford back to life. The Radford plant has been directed since 1985 by Eynon Thomas — a long-serving Jaguar man who took over from the even longer-serving Jack Randle (no relation of Jim). As with the body plant, the Radford engine and transmission factory has been thoroughly automated, so that

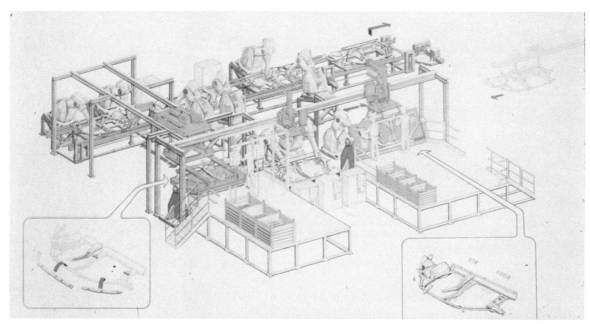

Later, 'C' Block was re-floored and refurbished to take the next stages of Jaguar's automated body manufacturing plan, examples of which are shown here diagrammatically.

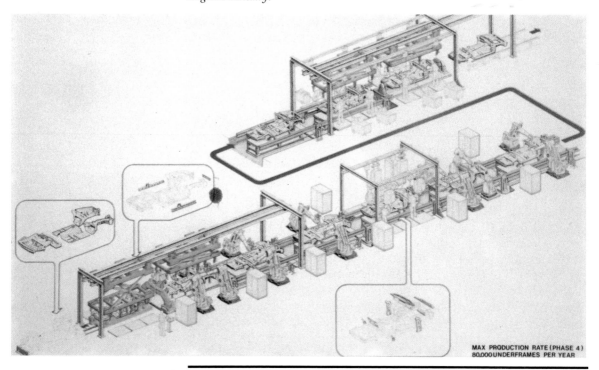

MAX PRODUCTION RATE (PHASE 4)
80,000 UNDERFRAMES PER YEAR

computer-controlled machines are the rule, not the exception.

At Browns Lane — directed by Walter Turner, a Jaguar man since 1954 — the decision to create a pilot-build facility made it possible to bring the XJ40 into production on the adjacent lines with minimum disruption. The first production line was commissioned during the 1986 summer holiday shutdown, and the second in the spring of 1987, when the last Series Three XJ6 was produced. The Series Three XJ12 would continue to be made at the rate of thirty to forty per week, utilizing the former XJ40 pilot-build area. (There were Daimler Double-Six and, confusingly, Jaguar Sovereign V12 versions of this model which, although not new designs, would provide the only immediate alternatives to BMW's V12 in the luxury sector.)

Traditional skills continue to be evident throughout the works. There are some things that automation cannot replace — nor would the company wish it. The selection and preparation of walnut and elm veneers and of cured hides for the passenger compartment remain exclusive to the craftsmen and craftswomen of Jaguar's own sawmill and trim shop. Customers around the world have made it clear that luxury, to them, means using the traditional materials which have always given Jaguars a unique, irresistable aura.

Pilot-build XJ40 line at Browns Lane, 1986. This was to be used for Series Three V12 production from 1987, releasing extra space in the main assembly hall to meet demand for the new model.

This picture and below
XJ40 final lines at Browns Lane.

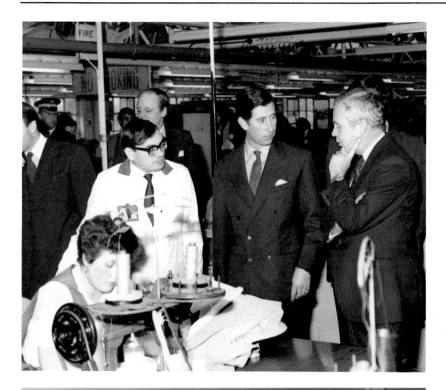

Traditional crafts still practised 'in-house' at Browns Lane include interior trimming, veneer matching and (for the Daimler limousine) cabinet-making — not just by Royal Command, but at the clearly-understood request of a majority of customers worldwide.

Before moving on to the pattern of progress, described in the following chapter, it is worth recording the unprecedented rate at which XJ40 production began during 1986.

Almost four hundred pre-production cars of various categories had been built by the end of May 1986. During the summer, the first production line was prepared. Below is a table of XJ40 production during the first four months, in terms of 'cars off the final line':

Week no.	Sept 1986	Oct 1986	Nov 1986	Dec 1986
1	41	123	272	244
2	101	191	261	321
3	188	159	285	340
4	98	169	286	114
5	(N/A)	280	(N/A)	(N/A)
TOTAL	428	922	1104	1019

So, with 3,473 XJ40s built in *series* production by the end of the year, Jaguar was setting new standards for itself. Production and profits are all-important in any industry and another achievement is therefore even more indicative of the new Jaguar company's resolve. Just occasionally during 1985, starting in April, a weekly output of one thousand cars was exceeded; the regular production schedule called for nine hundred plus. Within three months of its introduction, however, the XJ40 was contributing to a weekly figure of over one thousand. (The period in question was the last week of November 1986, in which 286 XJ40s supplemented the 718 other types which came off the final production line.) This made the 1987 production target of some 47,000 cars look quite feasible — another record for Jaguar but still only one tenth of BMW's output. Indeed, the German company looked set to go further on its successful way when its new Regensburg plant became operational, in addition to Munich and Dingolfing. There was no direct comparison, however, because Jaguar had moved out of the compact sports-saloon market in the late 1960s, when it put most of its eggs in the XJ basket, whereas BMW, scrambling out of a 1960 crisis, had moved firmly *into* that sector with its *Neue Klasse* saloons which have evolved into the 3-series and 5-series.

However, BMW's achievement has not been lost on Sir John Egan, even though he may not yet seek to produce half a million cars a year, or even 100,000. Nevertheless, he avoids resting on his company's many laurels, and his annual expansion rate of ten to fifteen per cent ensures that, before many more years are out, the Jaguar range will widen even further.

His achievements so far read thus:

Year	Personnel	Cars	Pre-tax profit of approx
1982	7,800	22,000	£ 10 m
1983	8,900	27,500	£ 50 m
1984	9,800	33,500	£ 90 m
1985	10,500	38,500	£120 m
1986	11,300	41,000	£120 m

Productivity may *seem* to have levelled-off by 1987, but it was in that year that the investment in automation and in the XJ40 was expected to pay off with significant increases in production but a levelling-off of manpower.

The graph on this page shows in simple terms how Jaguar production climbed in the 1950s, levelled off in the 1960s and took a bumpy ride in the 1970s — nearly hitting rock-bottom before the climb began all over again. This is, perhaps, the best way of illustrating that, in producing the XJ40, Jaguar has re-established true stability and competitiveness in the top luxury automobile sector.

Jaguar progress: passenger car output has generally progressed upwards since 1955, when the company's first modern 'compact' (the 2.4 saloon) was introduced. The sharp dip in 1972 was caused by a lengthy strike when Jaguar was having to negotiate to BL ground rules rather than its own. The second dip was a direct result of the OPEC oil crisis, and the deepest one of all relates to the change of paint facilities allied to quality problems of the late 1970s and early 1980s which the Egan regime has more than rectified.

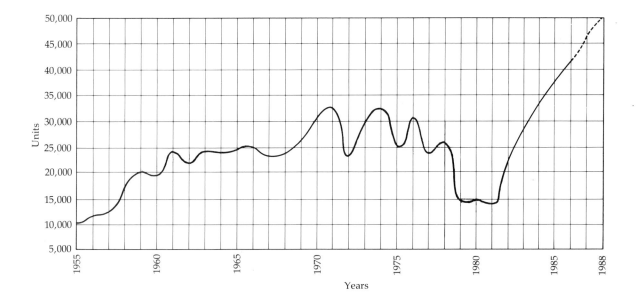

6

FIVE-YEAR PHILOSOPHY

This chapter reviews the five years leading up to the world launch of the XJ40 — the most significant new Jaguar for nearly two decades. These years are recorded in the form of highlight events and liberal quotations from Sir John Egan as addressed to his senior staff through Management Bulletins.

Apart from Egan's own message, which was often quite pungent, and always forthright, the bulletins contained confidential summaries on the status of manufacturing, sales and marketing, quality, finance, product engineering, purchasing and personnel. The latter area included employee relations, training and internal communications. Study of these bulletins provides intriguing insights into what was uppermost in Egan's mind at different times during this fascinating period of Jaguar history.

SPRING 1982
Although there were still many problems, by this time Jaguar people could look to the future optimistically. Egan wanted to make sure that the optimism was maintained without complacency creeping in, while the new-model programme gained momentum in parallel with that for the much-improved Series Three and XJ-S ranges.

Each of these monthly bulletins began with the chairman and chief executive's summary of the current situation. This backed up information on the company's performance in manufacturing, product quality and sales, which were always recorded in terms of target figures *versus* actual ones.

The first Management Bulletin was issued to cover Period 4 (April) in 1982, and these were John Egan's opening words: 'When compared with the situation eighteen months ago, the future for Jaguar is considerably more secure…However, we are not yet fully competitive with BMW and Mercedes-Benz.' He concluded, 'Communicating the contents of this Bulletin to your staff will further the feeling of community and assist the re-creation of the Jaguar Spirit.' This spirit may not be easy to define, but it was something generated by particular enthusiasm and particular achievement. Sir William Lyons had created it at Jaguar, giving his company an inner strength that had served it well; now John Egan recognized that spirit and rekindled it.

By the spring of 1982, production was exceeding 500 vehicles per week, well below the numbers achieved in the twelve-month period of October 1970 to September 1971 (Sir William's last full financial year in office, in which 32,589 cars had been delivered from Jaguar). It was, however, a significant improvement on the three preceding sales years in which output of motor cars from Browns Lane had dropped to a level not seen since the 1950s.

During April 1982, the first fully-engineered prototype (FEP) of the XJ40 structure was received from Pressed Steel-Fisher, and the work to make it mobile was begun. The test rig programme was well advanced by this time, and the new designated area was about to be occupied. Meanwhile, development of an Italian-made VM turbocharged diesel engine application (Project XJ59) appeared to be progressing well, although control of exhaust emissions in conjunction with Ricardo was presenting problems. The first AJ6 engines to go through the manufacturing process were delayed due to difficulties in producing acceptable cylinder head castings.

While most departments had been cutting down on staff, an ever-increasing workforce was causing Jaguar Engineering to burst at the seams, spilling over into a conglomeration of new 'kit' buildings. Lack of space in the old experimental department was eased when a new styling studio was completed. (The temporary nature of much of the new accommodation was accepted more readily later on, with the announcement of the complete removal of engineering to another site altogether.)

SUMMER 1982

There were echoes of Sir William's frustration in Egan's haranguings at this time. Quality and output were getting better all the while, but there was continuous fluctuation, too. 'I shall continue to talk about this until it is right, until every single Jaguar employee understands what is required by the Customer,' declared Egan. 'Only then will the future of our company be secure.' Video programmes were now a major feature of Jaguar's internal communications system, providing the opportunity to introduce everyone to the unlucky owner whose Series Three V12 saloon had spent one month (of its first four) in the repair shop; and he was just one example. 'This customer was surprisingly patient,' Egan told his management team. 'Many others could have chosen a BMW or a Mercedes-Benz instead. We have survived the last two years by hard work, determination, and a lot of luck. Exchange rates won't always be in our favour. We cannot sit back now. Relaxation will put us out of business.'

Positive action supplemented the words and, despite good progress, the XJ40 development programme was extended to ensure more built-in quality and reliability than the ever-improving current models possessed. (Nevertheless, 1984 was still the 'official' year of the car's release: to maintain the momentum, a traditionally optimistic target was retained until the genuine final countdown began.)

Renewed interest in the XJ-S (XJ27) became quite pronounced as the 2 + 2 coupé approached its seventh birthday. It had never been seen as a candidate for honours within the international racing formulae, although a North American Jaguar-sponsored team — Robert Tullius' Virginia-based Group 44 — had achieved national success. New in 1982, however, was a touring car race formula run under Federation Internationale de l'Automobile (FIA) jurisdiction, called 'Group A'. A British company — Tom Walkinshaw Racing (TWR) of Oxford — came up with a plan to make the Jaguar XJ-S competitive for this formula. In the recent past, the FIA's European Touring Car Championship had been for much-modified cars, but the Group A concept was to ensure certain basic similarities between production and racing models — a policy traditionally preferred by Jaguar.

At first, the company played down its interest; after all, Jaguar had been out of racing for many years. However, Egan did go on record enthusiastically in mid-1982: 'If we are to forge our way into the West German market, we must take a leaf out of Tom Walkinshaw's book,' he said. 'At the Nürburgring in early July the Team Motul Jaguar XJ-S took on and beat the BMW car. This is Tom's second win of the season after initial teething trouble and indicates that THE CAT IS BACK!' Indeed, those victories in the Brno Grand Prix and the German six-hour race had been worthy ones, for both circuits were considered to be among the most arduous in the world.

While this unexpected source of positive publicity was reaping its benefits, new variations on the XJ-S theme were being composed. The 'opus numbers' were XJ57 and XJ58, referring respectively to normal and cabriolet versions of the XJ-S in 3.6-litre six-cylinder (AJ6-engined) form, to be announced in the autumn of 1983.

AUTUMN 1982

Although it had not yet been abandoned for XJ40, the VM diesel engine project (XJ59) was shelved as an alternative power unit for the existing Series Three saloon due to unsatisfactory results in US testing. It is reasonable to suppose that, from a marketing point of view, the use of this type of engine would not have enhanced the marque's carefully-nurtured image.

The XJ40 itself underwent its first crash test, achieving all the legislative requirements and 'very good' injury criteria. As had been done with the XJ-S and the Series Three, task forces or groups were now established to control all aspects of the XJ40, with these as the priorities:

1. quality, reliability and driveability,
2. timing,
3. performance, economy and specification, and
4. cost.

Alford and Alder — a traditional supplier of suspensions — closed down as a BL company, and Jaguar acquired the relevant machines and equipment including heat treatment and plating plants. These were installed at the Radford, Coventry, factory where the AJ6 engine machining facility was also in the process of installation and commissioning.

The 'Price of Perfection' was the title given to a dealer conference in September, when over 200 franchise-holders came to Browns Lane to receive information on Jaguar's new hard-line sales manifesto. Egan's message to the dealers was simple: they must build quality into the preparation, presentation, sale and subsequent servicing of Jaguar and Daimler cars. He told them that some Jaguar customers were being given 'appalling' service according to a market research survey which had shown (among other things) that 69 per cent of potential owners were not being asked to leave their addresses. 'We at Jaguar are not prepared to have our efforts to succeed jeopardized by poor performance in the showroom,' he said. 'A bad dealer is worse than no dealer at all...Those who are not willing to join our unrelenting quest for perfection will lose their franchise...What I expect from our dealers is what I also expect from every Jaguar employee — **nothing but the best**.'

Big improvements in the quality of the body structures received at Browns Lane from the Castle Bromwich body and paint plant were commended from the top. However, Egan believed that the concentration of effort on improving that particular aspect had 'masked inefficiencies in many other areas which have repeatedly hidden behind the excuse that bodies have been in short supply'. Here he was blaming suppliers especially: within the company, Egan went out of his way to congratulate everyone in his Christmas message.

WINTER 1982–83

Testing of the XJ40 continued with increasing intensity. Another impact test in November was successful apart from the failure of a tank union caused by contact with the edge of the hole in the axle bridge panel through which it protruded; a modification was put in hand at once. Likewise, when an aluminium rear suspension pendulum failed after prolonged severe testing, a new specification for the component was quickly established.

The XJ40's suspension design was a crucial factor not only in road behaviour but also in the refinement which was essential to the modern Jaguar's character. Isolation of the rear spring seats, softer front suspension mounting bushes, and improvements to the aft engine mounting contributed to the new car's progress. December's Management Bulletin reported that 'harshness is now lower than in Series Three', adding that the XJ40 had already surpassed the existing models in its handling characteristics. Preparations for environmental testing in Canada were in hand, and by the New Year, 1983, two XJ40s were about to start around-the-clock running at Timmins, Ontario. Eight more XJ40s were running by now.

The 1982 production target of 21,000 cars had been exceeded, including an all-time record for North American sales of over 10,000, and Egan announced 27,000 as a minimum target for 1983. With the weekly supply of satisfactory structures now regularly exceeding 600, progress seemed good. However, as 1983 got under way, a falling-off of quality was noted once again — and once again Egan was on the warpath. Jaguar applied its own quality index system to several Mercedes-Benz and BMW cars, and found them consistently better; this would not do at all!

SPRING 1983

Surprisingly few major problems were encountered in the XJ40's Canadian winter testing, despite the 'handbuilt' nature

of the prototypes. Now, a further series of strenuous tests was being planned for other parts of the world. It was to be the most arduous testing programme in the history of Jaguar. (Quite independently, positive steps were being taken to establish a specification for XJ41 — Jaguar's projected sports car for the 1990s and beyond.)

Jaguar had had its own sales and marketing department for a year and on 3 April its most important single UK initiative was put into operation. This initiative took the shape of the Franchise Development Fund, which was established by the simple measure of reducing the dealer's discount from 18.5 to 15 per cent. The 3.5 per cent balance (based on the car list price) would be used to encourage dealers to invest in doing a good job for Jaguar. Basically, this meant employing Jaguar-only specialist staff; it was no good sharing with other franchises (and that included Austin Rover, too). It also meant treating the customer as an individual — providing him or her with the fullest service at every stage and not offering discounts. The Jaguar image must be built up, to provide business today and confidence in the XJ40 tomorrow.

That said, the Jaguar image *was* already improving. In North America, Group 44 gave its new mid-engined XJR-5 competition car — no relation to any production Jaguar apart from its basic V12 power unit — its first victory. In Europe, the TWR Jaguar XJ-S 'Group A' team now had official backing from Coventry. More than 500 Jaguar personnel attended the Donington Park 500 km race on 1 May, to see new star Martin

Winter testing of the XJ40 was based at Timmins, Ontario, Canada.

Brundle overcome the atrocious weather conditions to win. It was all part of the new team spirit.

SUMMER 1983

John Egan reported the first six months of the year as being 'encouraging' and 'excellent' in reference to quality and production respectively. His earlier concern about the German market was met on 20 June, when Jaguar Deutschland GmbH was formed with Zurich-based Emil Frey AG as the major shareholders. (Emil Frey himself had begun selling William Lyons' products back in 1926.)

The most important XJ40 engineering achievement was considered to be the successful testing of its front suspension in production form, as the early fabricated prototype suspension beams had been known to fail during the very severe pothole braking test. The production-type pressing, however, had now completed 130 stops (the normal standard was 50) without failure, and the vehicle remained safe to drive. (Indeed, the same suspension was transferred to a pavé test car for further tests.) It was also recorded that the rear suspension had completed 500 passes of the 'ladder' test plus more than 700 miles (1,100 km) on pavé. These achievements gave Jaguar's management 'very high confidence in the overall integrity and performance' of the structure.

At this time two XJ40s were shipped to Arizona for an eleven-week environmental test programme, and another went to the high-speed track at Nardo in southern Italy for sustained high-speed work. The US tests were satisfactory in most respects — especially those of air-conditioning, handling, cooling and fuel consumption. One car crashed, and although no one was hurt, the car had to be returned to the UK where it was written off.

The Nardo car completed 12,000 miles (19,308 km) virtually flat-out, its major problem being in the lubrication of the ZF automatic gearbox which had been chosen to replace the GM unit.

Quality and timing remained Jaguar's two most persistent day-to-day headaches. Instead of lecturing his team through the bulletin, Egan now chose to quote customers who had been interviewed by market researchers on the company's behalf. (Two hundred luxury-car users were being telephoned monthly, on average — and there were nine- and eighteen-month follow-up calls.) The results showed that, whereas nine out of ten Mercedes owners would buy again, only seven out of ten Jaguar owners would return to Jaguar. The difference was mostly put down to irritating small faults.

AUTUMN 1983

The surviving XJ40 Arizona prototype had completed the scheduled 25,000-mile (40,225-km) durability running and was now being updated in Canada for a 50,000-mile (80,450-km) cold climate 'sign-off' test. It would be joined by another prototype to replace the write-off; four more cars would also be sent to Timmins shortly, for tests running on into April 1984.

September saw the first four production-built XJ40s delivered, on time, to engineering; the next four were delivered in October, again on schedule. These vehicles were referred to as SDVs, or Specially Designated Vehicles.

The XJ57 and XJ58 were launched publicly at the Earls Court Motorfair, but represented (Egan told his management) 'a prime example of our inability to achieve model introduction deadlines. Fortunately we got away with it, but we cannot continue in this fashion. We are approaching the most important event (possibly) in the history of our company. All of our futures depend on the successful introduction of XJ40. We cannot launch it as just a name on announcement day. We must have cars in the dealers' showrooms, ready for our customers...As we continue along the tightrope to recovery, every year will be harder than the last; our targets will become greater as our competitors get tougher.'

WINTER 1983–84

With more than 27,000 cars built and sold in the calendar year, Jaguar had exceeded its original target for 1983 — but not the revised one, which had been set in the spring to cope with increased demand. 'We have missed out on the sales of 500 cars — the value of which is over £7,000,000 — and we may have lost anxiously-waiting customers to our competitors,' reported Egan, adding, 'We knew 1983 would be a tough year and the vast majority have got their heads down and achieved a great deal...Well done!'

An unsatisfactory crash-test performance in November led to minor modifications of the XJ40 and a totally successful re-test in December.

It was a severe winter in Canada, with temperatures down to −40°C in the Timmins region of Ontario where two FEPs (fully engineered prototypes) and four SDVs (specially designated vehicles) — including three 2.9s and three 3.6s — were accumulating the necessary high mileages despite the especially arduous conditions.

The first four UK SDVs began running in early November. Most major teething troubles were overcome soon after they had presented themselves. Hub bearings and Girling struts required modification as a result of the continuous high-speed pounding to which the cars were constantly being subjected. By this time, groups of employees from all three factories — Browns Lane, Radford, and Castle Bromwich — were being given the opportunity to drive and ride in the new vehicles which were, of course, still disguised.

SPRING 1984

After four years at the helm, John Egan was now able to talk of the company returning into the hands of private investors — a dream-come-true, especially for everyone who had seen the marque's pride eroded during BL's early years of state ownership. He told his management that the government would be making special arrangements to protect Jaguar's independence for some time to come, 'preventing our company from being purchased or controlled by any organization which might not have the best interests of Jaguar at heart'. (This 'Golden Share', which would keep individual voting shareholdings down to a 15 per cent maximum, was scheduled to remain in force until late 1990.)

These were optimistic days, with quality improving constantly and production heading for an all-time record of 33,000 cars, as planned.

XJ40 testing had exceeded half a million miles, and most basic problems had been solved by now.

SUMMER 1984

May, June and July saw Jaguar preparing to go private, and in the first week of August came the stampede for shares. This followed closely upon victory for the TWR Jaguar XJ-S in the Belgian 24-hour race, which extended what proved to be an unassailable lead for team leader Tom Walkinshaw in the European Touring Car Championship — a title he had only just failed to win in 1983.

By late summer more than a million XJ40 test miles had been completed, and the new vehicle endurance test facility in Phoenix, Arizona, was fully operational. Although the pressure was on to have the car ready in 1985, those who needed to know — like Jim Macaffer (director in charge of material control for production) — knew that autumn 1986 was now the practical launch target.

AUTUMN 1984

Just when everything was looking its best, a crisis reared its head. Details of a two-year pay deal had been communicated to

Jaguar's own permanent Phoenix base was set up by Richard Cresswell in 1983, and additional land was soon purchased to permit expansion. Double-shift running in Arizona's extreme conditions — plus annual test sessions at Pike's Peak and Death Valley — continue to provide Jaguar with invaluable data. On-duty members of the Phoenix team seen here are (left to right) John Heiple (right superintendent), Glenda Rumley, Jeff Paul, Theresa Wood, John Schantz, Margie Deppe, John Murchison (technical co-ordinator), Peggy Hunsaker, David Lees (Cresswell's successor in charge of the Phoenix outpost), Gene Rothenbush (day supervisor), Penny White, Tom Kee and mechanics Pete Perrone and Vic Brown. Facing the new XJ40 is the one with the highest mileage — SDV427 (a Phase Seven car) with close on 200,000 miles on the 'clock' by the spring of 1987.

the workforce — now approaching 10,000 in number again, having been forced down to 7,200 in 1982 by the lack of productivity — and on 25 October there was a mass meeting at which a strike decision was taken, after rejection of the company's final offer. A variation of the offer was turned down on 31 October, although by a smaller majority, and on 1 November the strike began. In an attempt to solve the deadlock, the company met trade union officials on 7 and 8 November, and offered another variation of the same offer which meant, in effect, that the basic rate was to be increased for Year One, but an equivalent amount would be lopped from Year Two. Peter had been robbed and Paul paid. A mass meeting on 9 November accepted the 'new' offer, and work began on the following Monday, 12 November. Seven working days had been lost.

This was Egan's first serious setback, and he was bitter about the losses — the loss of reputation and production for the company, and the loss of wages and bonuses for its people — but he never lost his own momentum and, very soon, he had put the incident behind him. (In the long run, it may have helped mutual understanding; Egan abhorred 'them-and-us' thinking.) 'We must knuckle down to two years' hard work, leading to the successful introduction of XJ40 which we shall not start to produce for sale until we are entirely confident that it is the best car in the world — which it will have to be to replace the Series Three XJ6 *and* compete with Mercedes-Benz.' By this time, however, the ideal theory (of not introducing the car until it was right) was tempered by the knowledge that the latest introduction date — autumn 1986 — must stay firm. It would be foolish to expect the Series Three XJ6 to sustain its popularity indefinitely.

A new engineering centre was needed urgently to accommodate the many additional functions that Jaguar required if it was to stay in business, let alone remain competitive, in modern industry. Browns Lane was sprouting more and more temporary buildings, and space was at a premium. It was welcome news for the engineers, therefore, that design work on their new centre (at Whitley, on the east side of Coventry) was well under way. They would move there from Browns Lane in 1987.

WINTER 1984–85

Nineteen eighty-four proved to be an all-time record year for the company, with 33,437 cars built and 33,355 cars despatched (the difference, in part, accounted for by the growing volume of pre-production XJ40s). The previous calendar year production record had been 32,478 in 1974; earlier still, in the financial year October 1970 to September 1971 inclusive, 32,589 Jaguars and Daimlers had been despatched. Although they were below target, due to the strike, the new figures marked a further step forward. Over 18,000 cars had gone to the USA and the favourable dollar/pound exchange rate was emphasized when pre-tax profits of more than £90 million were declared for 1984. (The financial and calendar years had been one and the same since 1976.) A sad note was struck by the death of Sir William Lyons, aged eighty-three, in February 1985.

Eight XJ40s completed a total of over half a million miles of testing during this winter, each car covering the 50,000 miles (80,450 km) required of it. Two of them were sent on to New York for city durability work, while the remaining six returned to Coventry for analysis.

Testing in Australia (using Sydney as first base) had been going on for a year, and by now it involved six cars; two of them had each completed 36,000 miles (57,924 km) on dirt-road durability runs, operating from Cobar.

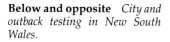

Below and opposite *City and outback testing in New South Wales.*

SPRING 1985

Production, quality and sales of the XJ-S range, now approaching its tenth anniversary, were better than ever, and the XJ27, XJ57 and XJ58 were about to be joined by the XJ28 — a V12-engined version of the two-seater cabriolet.

John Egan's themes were centred around leadership and 'getting the message across'. On the matter of internal communications he was insistent that his senior people should not only keep subordinates informed but be receptive to their ideas. It was natural to emphasize team spirit and loyalty from time to time, because there had been not only the dip in employee relations — causing the unnecessary strike — but also another dip in the quality index. 'Quality does not occur by accident,' said Egan. 'There is no doubt that our Quality Circles have been effective...but we must get **more** into operation to gain the full benefit of people's knowledge and suggestions. Japanese manufacturers have always been regarded as cheap imitators of their Western counterparts. Unfortunately the problem we now face, particularly in the motor industry, is that the copies are in many instances better than our originals...We

Above and opposite *Alex Frick organized testing in Oman to meet Middle Eastern customer requirements — and he took these pictures.*

must now learn a lesson from them.' These Quality Circles had been based on the Japanese way of obtaining commitment to the product through organized small groups. Now Egan was introducing another Japanese system (although it had originated in the USA): Statistical Process Control. This was the term for achievement of total consistency in production; its introduction was all part of the plan to set standards of manufacturing never previously achieved at Jaguar.

The main XJ40 news at this time was that most testing was running ahead of schedule, that Bosch had signed off the new Jaguar's antilock braking system equipment on time, and that 30 mph front and rear end crash tests had been successful.

SUMMER 1985

'By a great exercise of the Dunkirk Spirit, we survive; we now need the expert planning and dedication of the Normandy Landings to succeed.' That was John Egan's summer message. Soon afterwards, a half-year pre-tax profit of over £60 million was announced, and Egan called it 'good, but only just good enough'. There were many reasons why Jaguar should keep on its toes, such as the fluctuation in the value of the pound against the dollar, and the need to invest well, be more productive, and stick stubbornly to the new model programme. This is the way he put it to his top men: 'The British motor industry has a history of neglect and failure. We have proved so far that Jaguar is different; that we can survive and compete in a highly competitive professional environment. We must now prove that Jaguar has the ability to continue to grow, consolidate our position, and safeguard the long term future of the Company and our employees.'

For the second year in succession the American team, Group 44, brought a pair of its Jaguar V12-powered XJR-5 mid-engined cars to Le Mans for the 24-hour race. Neither had finished in 1984, although they had run well; the same could be said of 1985, only this time one of the cars was still running (in 13th place) at the end. It was the first time that a Jaguar-powered car had finished in this famous event for twenty-two years. Simultaneously, a British-built prototype World Sportscar Championship contender, the XJR-6, was readied for its first trials.

More than 20,000 cars were built by the end of June, setting yet another half-year record. During the July shutdown, work at the Castle Bromwich factory included a conversion to the Cathodic Electrocoat process of body treatment, to provide much-improved corrosion resistence. Pilot equipment was also installed for preliminary tests in anticipation of a switch to the use of a clear-over-base paint finish.

With just over a year to go, the XJ40's launch specification was signed off, the last item (late August) being the selection of the 2.9-litre automatic transmission model's final-drive ratio.

AUTUMN 1985

Already fully involved as shareholders themselves, employees were invited by an EGM Extraordinary General Meeting on 22 October to participate in a Jaguar savings-related share option scheme. 'We all share in the company's future. It is right that all who wish to do so should have a stake in that future,' said Egan. The same month saw Jaguar's major competition success of the year, TWR XJ-S coupés taking first and third places in the gruelling Australian 1000-km touring car race — the most publicized motoring event in the southern hemisphere. XJ-S worldwide sales continued to boom, as did the market for Series Three saloons. The XJ6 and XK-engined variants remained by far the most popular Jaguars, despite common knowledge that they would be obsolescent within a year.

Negotiations to purchase the former Talbot plant at Whitley, east of Coventry city centre, were nearing completion — giving Jaguar's engineers the certainty that they would be moving out of their somewhat fragmented accommodation at Browns Lane in 1987.

WINTER 1985–86

The appointment of Michael Beasley as assistant managing director was made, to enable John Egan to devote more time to his positions of chairman and chief executive. Derek Waelend replaced (and reported to) Beasley as manufacturing director. Beasley's contribution to the modernization of Jaguar's facilities and the improvement of its products — and thus to its reputation and profitability — made his appointment a natural one.

Production in 1985 easily exceeded all previous records at 38,000 plus, with over 20,000 cars going to the USA. (In December alone, a new monthly record was achieved when more than 3,000 cars were sold in the United States.)

By New Year 1986, some four million XJ40 test miles had been completed.

At a management conference in January, Egan declared Jaguar's objectives for 1986: to make 43,000 cars, with a productivity of 3.8 cars per employee; to improve quality in

'British' Jaguar Sovereign (seen in company with a classic Mark Seven and a 420G during the press assessment month at Glamis Castle) is identifiable by twin styled headlamps.

further specific ways; and to reduce the cost of materials from outside suppliers. 'If we can achieve all our objectives,' he said, 'Jaguar will leave behind the last remnants of the pre-privatization era and emerge as a world leader.' A major target for the new year was the reduction of warranty costs, and new procedures were laid down to pinpoint serious problem areas.

Pre-tax profits for 1985 exceeded £120 million — figures which were well received everywhere, and especially in the USA. With tax and dividends paid, this came down to £63.5 million — and the capital project programme estimate for 1986 was £94 million, including such essentials as modernization of paint technology and the development of computer aided design (CAD) in manufacturing and product engineering areas: Jaguar still had a lot of catching up to do, to match its rivals. No wonder Egan declared, '1986 is going to be one of the greatest challenges of all.'

SPRING 1986

The burning topic of the time was a reduction in the strength of the American dollar from a high of about $1.10 to the British pound a year earlier to something more than $1.50. It was a sign for Egan to designate special areas for significant improvement — all related to tighter budgeting allied to better performance. Following his declared policy of being receptive to ideas as well as producing them, Egan asked for an employee opinion survey. He described the early results as 'stimulating'. Of his knighthood, announced in the Queen's birthday honours list, he said that it had been earned by the efforts of everyone at Jaguar.

Group C (sports prototype) had replaced Group A (touring cars) as the priority in Jaguar's racing programme. Sponsorship from Gallaher International had led to the formation of the 'Silk Cut Jaguar Team', run by TWR — builders of the XJR-6 which scored its first victory in the Silverstone 1000-km race.

The XJ40 durability mileage was approaching five million by late spring, by which time preparations for the launch were well in hand.

SUMMER 1986

The July holiday saw one assembly track converted for production of the new car and, in August, 327 XJ40s came off the line, as had been scheduled for that month.

Despite the car's imminent announcement, Jaguar's total sales for the first six months of the year were 12 per cent up on those for the equivalent period in 1985, exceeding 20,000 units. By the end of August, 28,000 cars had been built during 1986.

In late August technical supremo James Randle master-minded the first engineering presentation of the XJ40. This was held at the London headquarters of the Institution of Mechanical Engineers. Between January and August, well over a million more durability test miles had been covered by prototypes, leading to a total of close on 5.5 million miles shortly before the launch date.

The American dollar remained fairly static, but the German mark had strengthened from 3.5 to just over 3 to the pound sterling — an adverse move when considered in terms of the increased sourcing of components in Germany, including both manual and automatic gearboxes for the new models.

AUTUMN 1986

'A landmark in automative history.' That was Sir John Egan's opinion of the importance of the XJ40 announcement on 8 October, following more than a month of press assessment testing, mostly in the Scottish Highlands. The car could be seen in all UK dealers' premises, and was substituted for the Series Three XJ6 at the Paris Salon. A week later, the XJ40 was the star of the British show, in Birmingham. Soon afterwards it was voted Top Car in a British press poll of thirteen new models, sponsored by the UDT finance house, ahead of the latest offerings from BMW and Mercedes-Benz. It came only fifth in the more international Car of the Year ratings shortly afterwards, where price and economy have become more dominant criteria.

WINTER 1986–87

Introduction of the new car had been the highlight of 1986 but, wrote Egan to his management, 'In terms of production and productivity we fell short of the mark with 41,000 units at 3.66 cars per employee against a target of 43,000 at 3.8 per employee'. Although infinitely better and more consistent than they had been in the bad times, quality targets were still not being met. Egan made no bones about it: 'It has taken us six years finally to shake off our poor reputation; it could take us just six months to get it back if our cars do not satisfy our customers' expectations.' Key objectives for 1987 included the manufacture of 51,000 units (minimum) with productivity of 4.2 cars per employee, plus specific reductions in the level of quality audit and first-year warranty faults.

Pre-tax profits of £120.8m for 1986 (as opposed to £121.3m in 1985) reflected the £11m spent on launching the new car. Improvements in equipment at all three factories (Browns Lane, Radford and Castle Bromwich) were proceeding well. Geoff Lawson and the styling team formed the 'advance party', occupying their section of the vast new Whitley engineering complex at New Year.

SPRING 1987

In April, the last XK-engined XJ6 (Series Three) saloons were produced, as the second main assembly line was turned over to the XJ40. Series Three V12 models should continue to be made in the former XJ40 pilot-build facility, while a new pre-production area (known as Track 7) was created to permit vehicles to be built prior to volume production without disruption of existing activities. Further updating of the engine manufacturing plant at Radford was matched by the refurbishment of 'C' block (the former Spitfire building at Castle Bromwich) for body-in-white automation. The body side robotic facility was already in full production, 'achieving all rate-of-climb requirements'.

The XJR-6 racing car gained a Design Council award for TWR, and by late May a new version (named XJR-8) had won four events and made best lap-time at the test-day held four weeks prior to the 24 Hours of Le Mans. Jaguar took a 20 per cent stake in a management buy-out of the Australian import company, which launched the XJ40 successfully in February despite a poor economic climate. The XJ40 was at the New York show in April and was launched on the US market in May — exactly sixty years after William Lyons showed his first ever Swallow-bodied Austin Seven in public.

Above *Curves characterized William Lyons' first Swallow saloon body design (seen here fitted to a Swift chassis) and continue to be a feature in the XJ40.*

Right *The well-known 'haunch' remains one of the strongest identifying features of the XJ40.*

Family resemblance: there is no doubting the heritage of the XJ40 when seen alongside the Series Three, but no body panels are inherited.

7

THE WRAPS COME OFF

Traditionally the launching of a new Jaguar has been a bonanza for the media...followed by frustration for the customer. It is healthy to have a long waiting list, of course, provided you can shorten it quickly and at the same time ensure that demand does not fall off. Sometimes it is a fine balance: if supply to some or all markets has to be rationed, credibility is maintained only if the product is known to be both desirable and reliable. Jaguars have always been desirable — but reliable? Less so.

Indisputably, many Jaguars of the past were launched before they were ready, as getting them on show and into production took precedence over engineering quality beyond the prototype stage. Jaguar was ahead in so many areas — including design engineering, style and value — but it fell short in other ways: notably in reproducing the best prototype's quality, time after time, on the production line.

In retrospect, the introduction of three new model ranges for the 1960s seems a super-human task; perhaps it was. The compact new 2.4/3.4/3.8 Mark Two range was an immediate success, from its launch in October 1959; it was based (*and* a big improvement) upon the 'guinea-pig' 2.4 which had been introduced four years earlier. By 1960, however, the sports cars and larger Jaguar saloons were showing their age and sales were slowing. Two new models — the E-type and the Mark Ten — were needed equally urgently. The E-type was fairly well developed when it was announced in early 1961 but, despite considerable testing compared with previous models, the Mark Ten was simply not ready when it was launched that autumn. Its early reliability problems tended to live with it in the public mind, even after its name was changed in 1966 — by which time it was a superb vehicle.

Many lessons were learned, and the translation of the original XJ6 to the production line was fairly successful, although it was a lengthy process.

Engineering for production has taken tremendous strides in the Egan era, however, considering that Jaguar entered the 1980s with dramatic quality and reliability problems — and these were not compatible with success. As Mike Beasley has said, 'John Egan had a simple mandate for Jaguar: fix it or shut it.'

Sir William Lyons, facing a slump in demand in 1958, wrote a message giving the three aims for the company — to keep prices competitive, to offer quality and finish comparable to the competition, and to make sufficient profit to invest in the future. When John Egan came on the scene in 1980, he switched the order of priority. Times had changed. Not only had Jaguar become psychotic, but the rest of the motor industry had become modern and sophisticated whereas BL had not. Moreover, the demand for foible-free motoring was now universal: the customer was concerned more and more with that than with initial cost. A quality product, modern technology to make it and *then* the right price — that was to be the new order of things.

Quality and technology preceded style as the XJ40's launchpads. The very sobriety of its still-so-Jaguar lines contrasted strongly with the dramatic, daring shapes which Sir William had released a quarter of a century earlier. The first XJ40 launch site was appropriate to the new-image Jaguar; yet there was also something quirkily different about it. Never had a complete motor car been seen in the main lecture hall of the Institution of Mechanical Engineers in Birdcage Walk, Westminster — never, that is, until the early hours of 28 August 1986, the day of the XJ40's first of many unveilings to an expectant world.

It was not just the location that made that London seminar unique. Certainly, it *was* an honour for Jim Randle, his XJ40 project leader Malcolm Oliver, and for the whole team to be allowed to present their new design in Britain's technical holy-of-holies.

There was also an aspect of the exercise which presented a challenge for the Jaguar experimental department's powers of improvisation. (These had been a key feature of Jaguar's working methods in the old days.) Everyone it seemed, except Jim Randle, had said that it would be impossible to get an XJ40 into the Institution. Randle declared that it *would* happen; and so it did, thanks to ingenuity in the design and construction of a special trolley with a rotating but removable cage. Without a doubt this piece of lateral thinking was therapeutic as well as

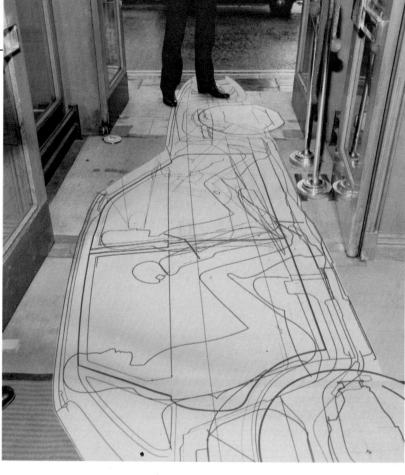

Above *Jim Randle at the Institution of Mechanical Engineers, London, for the Jaguar XJ40 presentation on 28 August 1986.*

Above right *The conundrum: would an XJ40 fit inside the Institution? No complete car had done so previously.*

Right *Nearly there: a serious Jim Randle directs operations.*

'Mission Impossible' is completed: the car stands on its wheels in the great lecture hall shortly before 3.30am. About to snatch a few hours sleep are (left to right) Colin Holtum, Stuart Spencer, Peter Ash, Dennis Peacock, Jim Randle, Jack Gee, George Mason, John Aldenton, Iain Young, Gerry Costello, David White and Randle's XJ40 project manager Malcolm Oliver.

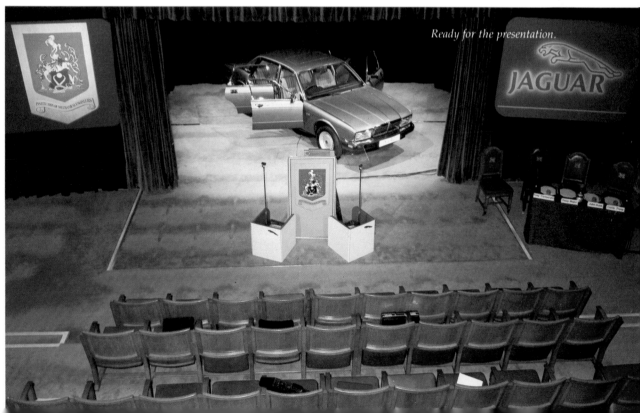

Ready for the presentation.

an engaging exercise for the Randle mind, so long stretched by the responsibilities which he had been shouldering quietly for six years, since taking over from Bob Knight.

The seminar itself was notable for the variety of papers presented, and for the way in which it became apparent that — at every stage — designers, and vehicle, component, manufacturing, and service engineers had worked together throughout, once the go-ahead had been given. There had also been much more outside consultation involving Birmingham and Loughborough Universities and other seats of learning. The effect of such a launch was to show that Jaguar truly cared that every customer would not only enjoy driving the XJ40; he or she could rely on it, as on no previous Jaguar.

The London seminar was followed by a whole series of presentations — not only to the press and the trade, but also to employees and their families at the National Exhibition Centre, Birmingham. The dealer events were held in the newly-enlarged headquarters building at Browns Lane, and were organized by Chris Baker of Jaguar, in conjunction with Cricket Communications, Birmingham. There were dramatic revelations, coloured lights and dry ice but, more important, there were people — people on stage, people on screen, talking stagily yet with infectious enthusiasm. It was not so much what they said that was impressive, but the way in which each audience was introduced to them personally; for this was no ordinary launch. It was an opportunity to show that Jaguar was being run once more by an expert, professional, determined, and enthusiastic team — in other words, by *Jaguar* people.

One of the most important presentations was for the North American dealers, for they would be selling more than 50 per cent of all Jaguars. Graham Whitehead (also a director of the parent company) and a fellow Britisher Michael Dale — Whitehead's second-in-command at Jaguar Cars Inc, USA — had used a mixture of diplomacy and ruthlessness to evoke true commitment from their dealer network while reducing the number of US dealers from 250 to little more than 150.

Chief link-man throughout these ninety-minute presentations was Roger Putnam, the sales and marketing director who had come to Jaguar in 1982 after many years at Lotus. (Incidentally, he was aware of Sir William Lyons' energetic efforts to merge Colin Chapman's company with Jaguar in the 1960s, only to be rebuffed after a deal had been struck.) Having built up a rapport with the audience, who had never been sold a new Jaguar with such dynamism, he introduced them finally to 'the man without whom the launch of XJ40 would not be complete', Sir

John Egan. The chairman confided in his listeners: 'For five solid years we have worked together, you and I, in preparation for the moment when we cross the threshold into the future...with the XJ40 we have re-created Jaguar design, engineering, and manufacturing as a world-class centre for automotive excellence...We have demonstrated that we can build, and will continue to build, the finest luxury saloon cars in the world today.'

This was no idle boast: before long, even the most critical of pressmen would find little with which to argue in Egan's claim.

As to 'five years' of co-operation; this was a specific reminder to his North American colleagues and dealers, eighty to ninety of whom had been flown to Britain in the summer of 1981, to see for themselves how Jaguar had changed for the better in little more than a year under Egan's rule. According to Dale, who had masterminded that exercise, 'They came filled with goodwill and sympathy, but without great expectations. They had a pre-conceived notion, based upon experience, that the British worker was not motivated, that the product and the parts delivery were poor. They went away with new hope. They also went away committed to taking the 9,000 Jaguars which John Egan said he could make for us in 1982.' In the event, over 10,000 Jaguars were supplied to the USA in 1982, and there had even been a further demand for the much-improved Series Three and XJ-S ranges.

By 1986 there had been many changes — but those dealers who remembered the 1981 meeting realized that Jaguar had kept its word. The cars *were* better than ever; volumes promised were volumes supplied; a model-year was looking more like a real model-year. It was a long time since that had happened.

While the static presentations continued in Coventry, dynamic ones were being conducted in the Scottish Highlands.

If you are going to present a new car to the public, you have to convince the press that it is worth writing about — and to achieve that, journalists need to handle it in all weather and road conditions. Fortunately, Central and Northern Scotland provide both — in attractive surroundings, *and* with relatively little traffic.

Until the 1970s, Jaguar had not been equipped with sufficient cars of production standard to provide this service. Even the XJ6 had had to be launched in 1968 with a minimum of vehicles available for driving on the road. The XJ12 of 1972 had been given a Swiss send-off — mainly because Jaguar needed a more 'European' image and because the Swiss motorways still had no official speed limit; but even then there had been only a handful of vehicles for the Zurich-based operation. In fact, the only Jaguar press previews ever to have provided a reasonable pre-announcement opportunity for journalists actually to road test the car had been for the Series Two XJ range, just before the first fuel 'crisis' of 1973 — and these previews had been held in Northern Scotland.

One key Jaguar engineer who had played an active part in ensuring that the quickly-conceived Series Two was ready for press appraisal (at least in four-door form!) was Peter Taylor, and he did the same again in 1979 when the Series Three appeared. His experience and his outspokenness in-house are not the only things that mark him out as one of Egan's most valued team members. 'When you're mentioning Jaguar people,' Sir John said to me, 'don't forget Peter Taylor. He's been an absolute hero. He has more feel for the car than the rest of us — an incredible knack of turning a great car into something even better.'

Taylor, like Richard Cresswell, Trevor Crisp, David Fielden, Malcolm Oliver and many other leading engineers, had been an apprentice of Jaguar Cars Ltd and had grown with the

Foreman John Coates in the self-contained temporary service workshop at Dunkeld during the pre-launch press sessions, Sept–Oct 1986.

Above *Jaguar's Dunkeld team of press-car engineers and fitters, September 1986. Left to right: John Sayer, Fred Nicklin, John Parsons, Frank Hydon, Aaron Mainwaring, John Coates, John Little, Martin McKeown, Gordon Gaskin and Ray Tallis.*

Left *The author in action in northern Scotland, September 1986.*

company. Jaguar has bred many an enthusiast, and Taylor is no exception; he raced his own V12 E-type successfully in the 1970s. This Browns Lane sporting trait probably comes with the territory; in Taylor's case it was an inevitable development, for he spent the final year of his apprenticeship in the vehicle proving department — now Cresswell's responsibility, and then run by the legendary Norman Dewis. His experience of vehicle proving began in 1966 when the pavé testing of the original XJ6 (XJ4) was taking place. So, when it came to choosing over which terrain the XJ40 might best demonstrate its special characteristic, it was natural for the public affairs director David Boole and product affairs manager Colin Cook to involve Peter Taylor in selecting the best available route.

Ideally, a press-test route should be long enough and interesting enough to make appraisal possible. For the XJ40 it was decided to go further and create one with poor surfaces and hazards such as sharp and even abnormal bends, cambers, and humps. This confidence in the new car might have seemed misplaced — but it was all part of Egan's bullet-biting principle. He and Jim Randle and Trevor Crisp drove the cars around the selected circuit (which included some of Scotland's highest and trickiest through-roads), took a gulp or two, and then approved it. Their approval would result in the approval of cynical, hard-driving journalists who, in trying to find an Achilles heel in the XJ40's handling and braking, could not help but be more impressed than they had expected. A softer option could have been found, to ensure that first impressions were good, but selecting a challenging route was one more, if small, example of the new-look Jaguar organization in action, and it brought its rewards in editorial coverage on and after 8 October 1986. The generally-fine autumn weather was a bonus which no one could have anticipated.

Jaguar's emphasis on teamwork was proved publicly on the evening of 7 October, when every one of the UK dealerships had a Jaguar director or senior manager on hand to introduce the new car to customers. The British dealer network was now operating on a single-tier basis, and was carefully organized geographically. Just over one hundred highly-specialized outlets now handled the Jaguar and Daimler marques, and the maximum number which could be run by any one company was three. (In the USA, prevention of monopoly was even stricter: only one Jaguar dealership could be owned by any single corporation.) Sir John Egan presented the car at Stratstone's, the traditional London agents for Daimler, with close Royal connections.

Still under wraps — just before the Paris Salon unveiling, October 1986.

Announcement-day headlines are studied by sales and marketing director Roger Putnam en route to the Paris Show, 8 October 1986. Accompanying him are (left to right) Stephen Perrin, marketing director, Barry Thrussell, service director, and John Morgan, European sales operations director.

Announcement day itself was 8 October. This was part-way through the Paris Salon, one of the major autumn motor shows, where Alan Hodge had masterminded a quick overnight switch of two of the exhibits. He kept the two XJ40s that he had 'smuggled in' under wraps until mid-morning, when a press conference was held by the recently-appointed French importer, with Roger Putnam, John Morgan, Barrie Thrussell, and Stephen Perrin on hand to represent Jaguar. Soon afterwards came Britain's own motor show, of which the XJ40 was the undisputed star.

Although he professed not to be concerned about international polls, Sir John Egan shared a general sense of wonder at the result (and purpose) of the 'Car of the Year' award; and many features were written subsequently expressing mystification at the relatively poor placings of both the Jaguar and its natural rival, the new BMW 7-series, in such a contest. British journalists, voting for the 'Top Car' nomination, gave the XJ40 that accolade, however, which was some consolation — especially as BMW and Mercedes-Benz took second and third places.

By the end of the year, the new car had been introduced into the major European and Middle Eastern markets, and February 1987 saw its arrival in Australasia where so much of the pre-production testing had taken place.

Jaguar's biggest market is North America, and it was only natural that the XJ40's biggest send-off should be here. If it were not for the United States, there would be no place at all for a car

Press day at the British motor show, October 1986, featuring (left) Jaguar engineer Peter Taylor.

After a fine autumn, the winter of 1986–87 was a good test of the XJ40's corrosion-proofing of which much was expected but little should be heard for many a year. This salt-caked Daimler was photographed in Norfolk.

Australian journalist Les Hughes with an XJ40 during press testing in Queensland, February 1987.

Above opposite *The directorate of Jaguar Cars Inc, responsible for the sale and service of more than half of all Jaguars built, in attendance at their Tampa, Florida, dealer convention in March 1987. Left to right: Dale Gambill, parts; Bob Burden, marketing; Sam Tucker, sales operations; Ray Polakoski, service; Graham Whitehead, chief executive; Mike Dale, senior vice-president; and Edward McCauley, finance. (Tom McDonnell, PR, is missing.)*

Below *'Jaguar XJ6: A Species Refined': from the American launch brochure.*

of Jaguar's style, price and engineering integrity. '*This* is Jaguar's home market!' declared Gene Fisher, head of the US Jaguar dealer council, emphatically, and who would care to argue with him? Since 1982, well over fifty per cent of all new Jaguars had been sold there.

Gene Fisher's statement was echoed time and again at the Tampa, Florida, dealer convention in March 1987, organised by Roy Gordon of Jaguar Cars Inc and attended by the directors of Jaguar plc with Graham Whitehead, Mike Dale and their colleagues as hosts. Dale's hard-line policy with the dealer network appeared to have paid off. 'Ours must be the only company that brags about a downward graph,' Dale joked, referring (in his pre-launch presentation) to the efficiency and profitability that must come from having a smaller but much sharper sales network. He brought plenty more good news, too. The mileage limit for 'Select Edition' — claimed to be the only genuine pre-owned car-sale scheme to carry a factory warranty — would be increased from fifty to sixty thousand miles (*applause*). Moreover, an 'SOS' service would apply to all 1988 models (*more applause*). Jaguar Cars Inc's service chief, Ray Polakoski, elaborated on this commitment for quality: SOS or 'service on site' promised that, in the event of a vehicle

Introducing the New Breed Jaguar XJ6

Sir John Egan and the XJ40, centre-stage at Tampa dealer convention, March 1987.

breaking down, the customer would be transported by the quickest possible means to his or her planned destination (and kept mobile) while the offending vehicle was repaired and then taken to the user's chosen location. It was difficult to image a more customer-oriented roadside rescue service.

If the US dollar was not as favourable as it had been, prospects for Jaguar-style motoring in the USA remained favourable, as JCI's newly-appointed head of marketing, Robert Burden, explained demographically. (Bob Burden had worked with Whitehead and Dale before, but BMW had been taking advantage of his special skills in recent years.) By demographics, trends become statistics which can influence marketing. As an example, Burden pointed out that, *daily*, the centre of US population moves 58 feet west and 29 feet south, 13,000 babies are born and 5,700 people die, 13,300 people get married and 6,500 divorce. Burden's main point, however, was to highlight the increasing average age (as well as affluence) of the potential Jaguar buyer, for the products of the post-war baby boom were now approaching middle age. The potential new clientele for Jaguar appeared to be spread across a wider spectrum than ever, quite apart from the return of a number of 'defectors' who had abandoned Jaguar not so much because of the days spent 'off the road' but rather as a result of the ribald jokes of neighbours or colleagues.

While the US and Canadian dealers were receiving their final briefings in Florida, JCI's Mike Cook was putting the finishing

1988 model year dealer show, Florida, 1988, attended by Jaguar plc's directors and the Jaguar band.

Left *Jaguar Vanden Plas near Tucson, Arizona.*

Below *Press test routes in Arizona included innumerable sharp dips, designed to cope with flash-flooding. No cars were damaged, despite hard driving.*

Jaguar men at Tucson for the US press presentation, March 1987. Left to right: Peter Taylor, Mike Dale, Jim Randle, Sir John Egan, David Boole, and Malcolm Oliver.

touches to the press launch in Arizona, where road conditions vary from long, straight desert highway to twisty, mountainous terrain with frequent sharp dips to cope with the rare but inevitable flash-flooding which can wash away an ordinary bridge. After completion of this phase, the final US countdown began at New York's show in April.

Meanwhile, Sir John Egan flew on to Japan, where a new company, Jaguar Japan KK (60% owned by the Seibu Group and 40% by Jaguar) launched the XJ40 amid growing tension between Britain and Japan over trade barriers. Although it was going to take time, the medium-term aim was to sell five thousand Jaguars in Japan annually through approximately twenty exclusive dealerships. Evidently, the Jaguar mystique had returned — and it was as intangible as ever.

In the XJ40, Jaguar was producing a car that was fast approaching Japanese and German standards of manufacture, but no-one else, it seemed, could reproduce that peculiarly British quality which Sir William Lyons had begun and which Sir John Egan and his team had re-established — CHARACTER.

Moreover, by the late 1980s Jaguar was becoming more outward-looking. A particularly happy example of this was an initiative (by John Mackie, head of Jaguar's Canadian operation) to help protect the magnificent beast which has given the marque its name. Truly, Jaguar is preserving as well as evolving the species.

The US-spec press car fleet of XJ6 and Vanden Plas sedans which performed so well at Tucson in March 1987.

Uncharacteristic weather affected the Arizona press tests.

APPENDIX

EVOLUTION OF
THE SPECIES

1922: Lyons is twenty-one on 4 September; his partnership with William Walmsley, sidecar maker, is ratified one week later with the formation of the Swallow Sidecar Co, 'in the trade or business of Body Manufacturers for Motor Sidecars', at 5 Bloomfield Road, Blackpool. Swallow sidecars are displayed at the London motor cycle show, 25 November to 2 December.

1923: Harry Teather and Arthur Whittaker join Swallow. Additional premises rented.

1924: First racing successes: three Swallow outfits start in the Isle of Man sidecar TT, and finish second, third and fourth. William Lyons marries Greta Brown.

1925: Alice Fenton becomes Lyons' secretary.

1926: Lyons orders an Austin Seven chassis. The Swallow Sidecar (and Coachbuilding) Co moves into bigger premises in Cocker Street, Blackpool.

1927: The Austin Seven chassis is invoiced to Lyons on 21 January. The Austin-Swallow two-seater is announced in *The Autocar* on 20 May.

1928: An Austin-Swallow saloon prototype is built. Car production capacity is limited to two cars a day, so a large Henly order hastens the company's move in October–November from Blackpool to a larger factory in Coventry.

1929: Swallow coachwork is displayed on Fiat,

William Lyons, aged 20, with the Swallow sidecar he bought from his neighbour, William Walmsley, the man who was to be his partner from 1922 to 1934.

The first all-steel SS Jaguar, completed in late 1937 and shipped to Romania for King Carol.

Standard, and Swift chassis at the October Olympia Motor Show, London. Wall Street 'crashes' in the same month.

1930: The company builds up production of sidecars, and Austin Swallows in particular.

1931: Introduction of the first SS range, with the cooperation of the Standard Motor Company. On 9 October, the *Daily Express* describes the £310 SSI coupé as the car with 'the £1,000 look'.

1932: An improved SSI establishes SS as a marque offering real style at a bargain price.

1933: SS Cars Ltd is incorporated on 26 October, reg. no. 280990.

1934: Walmsley gives notice of his resignation from the partnership at the first AGM of SS Cars Ltd on 28 November.

1935: New York's Mayor La Guardia opens the motor show in Grand Central Palace on 5 January; MG and SS are the only British makes. On 10 January, London's *Financial News* announces details of the flotation of SS Cars Ltd as a public company with capital of £250,000, and Lyons as the majority shareholder. William Heynes joins SS as chief engineer in April. Lyons fails in an attempt to buy the 'Sunbeam' car business. He announces his new SS 'Jaguar' range on 24 September.

1936: An SS Jaguar 100 sports car makes best performance in the International Alpine Trial.

1937: Over 3,500 SS cars are produced in the financial year to 31 July. New 3.5-litre models and steel body structure are introduced for October's motor show. A new reg. no. 333482 is incorporated on 9 November, and called 'Jaguar Cars Ltd' (but it is not used for trading).

1938: SS Jaguar 100 sports cars win more events, including the RAC Rally for the second year in succession. Walter Hassan joins the company's engineering team.

1939: The neighbouring Motor Panels company is bought secretly with a view to controlling steel body production. Over 5,000 cars are produced in the financial year ending 31 July. War in Europe.

1944: As war draws to a close, the Swallow sidecar

business is sold to the Helliwell Group; Motor Panels is sold to Rubery Owen, as it has not proved easy to integrate. Lyons tells *The Motor World* (17 Nov) that SS Cars Ltd means to expand and that 'manufacture will be concentrated upon cars of even higher quality than in the past'; also that 'it is intended to take full advantage of export markets' after the war.

1945: Lyons announces that 'Jaguar' is to become the marque name. SS Cars Ltd becomes a 'paper' company (reg. no. 333482) while Jaguar Cars Ltd takes over the number 280990 from SS to become the operational company on 9 April. Post-war car production begins in August.

1946: In May, Bill Heynes (chief engineer) joins Lyons, Thomas Wells Daffern (Coventry Permanent Building Society) and Arthur Whittaker (general manager) on the board of Jaguar Cars Ltd. Raymond 'Lofty' England (35) arrives at Swallow Road as service manager in September.

1947: Left-hand driving position is now offered. Nearly a quarter of the production is exported.

1948: Introduction of the 'XK' double-overhead-camshaft six-cylinder 3.4-litre engine; the XK120 sports car is shown at the first post-war London show in October.

1949: XK120 sports cars finish first and second in the inaugural *Daily Express* production car race at Silverstone in August.

1950: Jaguar's tentative début at Le Mans with the production-model XK120 is followed by victories in the Alpine Trial and Ulster TT race. Walter Hassan leaves to join Coventry Climax. The XK-engined Jaguar Mark Seven is described by *The Autocar* as the 'Prima Ballerina' of the London show in October.

1951: First stages of a move from Swallow Road, Coventry, to larger and better manufacturing facilities at Browns Lane, are undertaken. The new Jaguar XK120C (or C-type) competition model scores a sensational début victory in the Le Mans 24-hour race, and then the Ulster TT, while XK120s make best performance in the French (Alpine), Belgian (Marathon de la Route), Dutch (Tulip), and British (RAC) rallies.

1952: The move to Browns Lane is completed. Jaguars begin winning races using disc brakes. An XK120 coupé averages more than 100 mph (160 km/h) for a whole week and breaks several world speed records. Another record is achieved with close on 9,000 cars produced in the financial year ending 31 July (8,000 being for export). C-types begin winning races in the USA.

William Lyons and western USA agent Chuck Hornburg with one of their staunchest Hollywood customers, Clark Gable, and an XK120.

1953: C-type Jaguars are victorious in the Le Mans, Reims, and Hyères endurance races. Jaguar production is now running at over 10,000 cars a year for the first time. Automatic transmission is adopted.

1954: The XK140 sports car replaces the XK120; the D-type competition model replaces the C-type and wins the Reims 12-hour race. A Jaguar Cars North America Corporation is formed in New York, run by Johannes Eerdmans. Trevor Crisp begins his Jaguar apprenticeship.

1955: D-types win at Sebring and Le Mans. William Lyons' only son is killed in a road accident. Jaguar enters the 'compact' market with a monocoque 2.4-litre saloon in September.

1956: William Lyons is knighted in the New Year Honours. His deputy, Arthur Whittaker, picks his moment at the 5 January board meeting to ask Lyons whether he has given thought to issuing special shares to employees; Lyons promises to consider the idea. A works Mark Seven saloon takes outright victory in the Monte Carlo Rally. After over thirty years with the company, Alice Fenton is appointed director of home sales. In October, Jaguar announces its withdrawal from direct participation in racing. David Fielden begins his Jaguar apprenticeship.

1957: A large section of the factory is destroyed by fire on 12 February but production is resumed quickly, and the announcement of a new high-performance saloon (the 3.4) goes ahead a fortnight later, as planned. The disc-braked XK150 follows in May. A factory-prepared Ecurie Ecosse D-type with fuel injection gives Jaguar its fifth Le Mans victory (and the Scottish team its second in succession). The first E-type prototype is tested this year, which is another record one in production terms despite the setback caused by the fire.

1958: Jaguar output leaps forward again — this time to nearly 18,000 cars in the financial year, thanks to construction of post-fire facilities.

1959: A confusingly-named 'Mark Two' version of the compact Jaguar range is introduced in October with a choice of 2.4-, 3.4-, or 3.8-litre engines; disc brakes are standard. Production for the year exceeds 20,000 cars for the first time. [*Jaguar always made a profit as an independent company; this year saw it pass £1 million after tax — another 'first'.*]

1960: Home sales director Alice Fenton (49) dies suddenly; Sir William says, 'I have lost a colleague and a friend'. The purchase of the Daimler Company from BSA (Birmingham Small Arms) permits expansion within Coventry, rather than elsewhere. It also

Jaguar acquired Daimler in 1960, and continues to market the famous name. Here Sir John and Lady Egan tackle the 1986 London–Brighton Run in an early example.

allows Jaguar to diversify into military vehicles and buses, and to perpetuate Britain's oldest 'living' make of car. A Daimler truck is conceived.

1961: The modern age of Jaguar begins with the launch of the sensational E-type at the Geneva show in March, followed by the big Mark Ten ('Zenith') towards the end of the year. Both cars feature fully-independent suspension as well as disc brakes, and in their respective fields they set new standards of ride, and reduction of noise and vibration. Wolverhampton commercial vehicle-maker Guy Motors is bought by Jaguar from the receiver for £800,000, and Daimler's truck project is transferred there.

1962: Chief accountant Arthur Thurstans joins Lyons, Whittaker and Heynes on the Jaguar Group board which — since 1961 — has included John Silver (production), Robert Grice (works), and Raymond England (assistant managing director). S.E. Aston (ex-Daimler) becomes company secretary on the death of long-serving E.F. Huckvale.

1963: Coventry Climax Engines Ltd joins the Jaguar Group, thus bringing the celebrated engineer Walter Hassan back into the Jaguar fold. Driving 3.8-litre saloons with German Jaguar importer Peter Lindner, Peter Nöcker wins the inaugural European Touring Car Championship. Project XJ3 (or 'Utah Mark Three') is introduced as the Jaguar S-type saloon.

1964: Sir William Lyons reports talks with Colin Chapman to his board in April, declaring

Lotus to be 'a good little business' with 'young and capable management', plus prospects of expansion. In December however, he says that the deal will not go ahead, due to Lotus' 'rejection of our proposals, to which they had previously agreed'. In this month, Lyons makes his last significant acquisition for the Jaguar group — Henry Meadows Ltd, Guy Motors' next-door neighbour. Autumn sees the launch of a successful range of heavy-duty trucks and tractor units — the Guy Big J (or 'Big Jaguar'). The E-type and Mark Ten go up from 3.8 to 4.2 litres, and receive a new all-synchromesh gearbox. Harry Mundy joins the Jaguar engineering division.

1965: The saloon car for the future, Project XJ4, is well advanced, with plans for Jaguar V12 *and* V8 power units. James Randle joins the Jaguar engineering team. Coventry Climax engines take their fourth Formula 1 World Championship.

1966: At Geneva in March the notable Italian coachbuilders Bertone and Frua display handsome 2+2 coupés based on the 3.8-litre S-type saloon's running gear, supplied by Jaguar; the Bertone car is brought to Coventry where engineers drive it and report favourably. The board's report states that its sales potential is considered good, and the newly-appointed director and company solicitor Alan Newsome is asked to prepare a draft contract with a view to manufacture. A possible return to racing is also considered by the board in June. Lyons' privately-arranged

The 1966 Jaguar 3.8 S-type Bertone FT show car, which was being considered for limited production until mergers led to new priorities at Jaguar.

Sir William Lyons and Bill Heynes with the original XJ6, as launched in 1968. Many of those in the picture were also involved in designing and developing the XJ40. Notables in the foreground include Bob Knight, Norman Dewis, Jim Randle, Keith Graham, Tom Jones, Malcolm Sayer, Fred Gardner, Claude Baily, Gerry Beddoes, Bert Tattersall, 'Doc' Tait and Ted Addy.

merger of BMC and Jaguar becomes public knowledge with an announcement at the Riverside Suite of London's Grosvenor House Hotel on 11 July. The Bertone car and motor racing are put aside at the August board meeting. Project XJ16 (Jaguar 420) is introduced this autumn; the Mark Ten is revamped as the 420G at the same time.

1967: On 10 January Sir William Lyons discusses the future with his fellow directors, and asks them to give thought to the 'succession'. The Jaguar group shows a post-tax profit of more than £1 million (as it has done for nearly a decade) in this its last year of fully independent accounting.

1968: At New Year, Sir William Lyons announces his intention to remain Jaguar's chief executive and chairman, but to make Robert Grice (nearing retirement) and Raymond England (56) joint managing directors. A plan to merge British Motor Holdings (BMC plus Jaguar) with Leyland is also announced in

January. The Jaguar board hears from Lyons in February that Project XJ4 includes the possibility of Vanden Plas developing a drophead coupé version; limousine development with the same company is 'progressing well'. (The XK-engined Daimler limousine will be announced in June.) At the March board meeting publicity chief Robert Berry is called in to discuss the launch and naming of Project XJ4. A model *name* as such is not favoured: 'XJ6', 'XJ8', and 'XJ12' are preferred. The British Leyland Motor Corporation begins to operate on 14 May. At Jaguar's June board meeting it is decided to 'defer' the V8- and V12-engined cars until after the production plant is in full operation. In September, Project XJ4 is announced as the 'XJ6', and goes on to win numerous accolades. A planned two-door version is postponed, due to the high price being quoted by Pressed Steel-Fisher. Deputy chairman Arthur Whittaker retires, following a long illness.

Richard Cresswell driving a prototype XJ6 hard in Wales in about 1967 or 1968. Cresswell has been deeply involved in XJ40 testing, too.

Jaguar's technical overlord from 1935 to 1969, Bill Heynes, and the most famous sports car of all — the E-type. A new Jaguar sporting model is being planned for the 1990s by Jim Randle and his engineering team.

1969: Bill Heynes is awarded the CBE and retires as vice-chairman, engineering, in July, when Walter Hassan and Robert Knight are appointed board directors representing Jaguar power unit and vehicle engineering respectively. Project XJ27 (later XJ-S) is now receiving considerable attention at board level.

1970: At the January board meeting, Knight expresses concern at Pressed Steel-Fisher's rearranging its programme, as complete XJ27 body tooling cannot now be anticipated before 1972: 'The need for this to be not later than the spring of that year is stressed, as it is felt that it may be difficult to continue the present E-type as an acceptable car by that time'. In March, England says it is intended to present Project XJ25 (general term for the Series Three E-type) 'at the next London show, *and* have 250 in the USA at announcement'.

1971: XJ25/26 (E-type Series Three coupé and roadster) is announced in late March, to prolong the life of the E-type, and effectively test the Jaguar V12 engine. A new Jaguar five-speed gearbox is proving satisfactory in three cars so fitted. Jaguar (in trouble with its 2.8-litre version of the XK engine) successfully withstands BL pressure to use the Rover V8 engine. Arthur Thurstans retires and David Jenkins succeeds him as finance director. The first XJ27 (XJ-S) body is expected 'by the end of November', when costs of producing a 'slant-six' engine are also assessed. Sir William Lyons and Harry Mundy attend the US launch of the V12-engined E-type at Palm Springs. Graham Whitehead takes over the US operation from Johannes Eerdmans. In this financial year, ending 30 September, 32,589 cars are delivered from Browns Lane — an all-time record not to be beaten until 1984.

1972: At his final full board meeting as chairman of Jaguar Cars Ltd, on 8 February, Sir William Lyons (70) expresses his continual concern at the cost of running the business. He confirms to those present — Messrs Aston, England, Grice, Hassan, Jenkins, Knight, Newsome, and Rosenthal (manufacturing director, ex-Meadows), but not Stokes — that he is retiring on 3 March. Walter Hassan, the oldest serving board member, says how much he has enjoyed working for Sir William and makes several more remarks which 'represent the feelings of the board'. Raymond England becomes chief executive and chairman on

Monday, 6 March. In the spring, Knight investigates 'XJ27 open car' possibilities in relation to US definitions of a convertible. A 3.4-litre replacement for the 2.8-litre version of the XK engine is progressing. Grice and Hassan retire, the latter having stayed on until the age of sixty-seven to see the V12 engine into production. The XJ12 is announced in the summer, closely followed by long-wheelbase saloons produced quickly to scupper the Rover P8. England opens the 4 September board meeting by pointing out that it is Sir William's seventy-first birthday and therefore the fiftieth anniversary of the company's operations. (A special exhibition has been held in Coventry all summer.) An '**XJ40** Project' meeting takes place between England and Knight. Jaguar Cars Ltd ceases to be the operational name from 1 October.

1973: On 27 March a series of company changes takes place: 280990 (Jaguar Cars Ltd) becomes British Leyland Exports Ltd and in due course will become BL International Ltd. 851641 (Jaguar Exports Ltd) becomes Jaguar Cars Ltd, then Leymotor Five Ltd. The Series Two XJ6 and XJ12 are announced and a full-size **XJ40** styling model is shown to BL management. Geoffrey Robinson is appointed to run Jaguar in the autumn, with England staying on as non-executive chairman of a Jaguar division of British Leyland. Purchase director Harry Teather retires after fifty years with the company. A voluntary 10 per cent cut in fuel usage is adopted in most industries in mid-October, signifying the start of the first world oil crisis. On 20 November a voluntary 50 mph speed limit is introduced in Britain; on 29 November petrol coupons are issued, and on 7 December the 50 mph limit becomes law for a minimum of four months.

1974: Raymond ('Lofty') England retires in January, aged 62, finding the non-executive chairmanship unworkable alongside chief executive Geoffrey Robinson, 34. (Bones of contention include the temporary shelving of the Series Two XJ two-door coupé soon after its public announcement, plus a BL decision to get two completely new **XJ40** styling exercises done in Italy.) In February Robinson brings in three new directors from Ford, retaining only Robert Knight (engineering) and Alan Currie (sales) from the former Jaguar board. The Browns Lane and Radford plants are,

however, being run by two long-serving Jaguar men, Peter Craig and Jack Randle. High production, despite a three-day week, is offset by poor quality. Robinson's plans for major expansion are halted by government intervention in British Leyland's affairs. Sir Don Ryder's BL investigation team is appointed on 18 December.

1975: The last E-type deliveries are made. British Leyland's top management stands down. The Ryder Report, published on 23 April, results in the abolition of an individual Jaguar management board and Robinson resigns. (BLMC's top men, Lord Stokes and John Barber, also go.) Under 'Leyland Cars', a Jaguar 'operating committee' is not allowed to operate. The XJ-S is announced in the autumn when, for the first time, Jaguar is forced to share its UK motor show stand with 'Leyland' cars. The best news of the year is Robert Tullius' victory with the obsolete E-type in a North American racing championship.

1976: Jaguar morale hits rock-bottom, as its two major plant chiefs report to different areas of the loss-making corporation. Many executives leave Leyland, among them John Egan, the man who has built up one of its few successful operations — Unipart; he takes a top job at Massey-Ferguson. Jaguar's engineers continue their work on current and future projects including the **XJ40**, thanks to Bob Knight's refusal to report to anyone else but Leyland Cars' chief, Derek Whittaker.

1977: Peter Craig dies suddenly and is succeeded (as director of the Browns Lane factory) by Michael Beasley, aged thirty-three. Robert Knight receives a CBE in the New Year Honours list. **XJ40** is called 'LC40' within Leyland Cars, but not in the depths of Knight's department. On 1 November Michael Edwardes takes up his appointment as British Leyland's fourth chairman since Lord Stokes' departure. Edwardes' plan is (he writes later) 'to devolve authority...and put much greater responsibility back where it belongs — at the operational level'.

1978: Edwardes instigates the separation of Leyland Cars into Austin Morris and Jaguar Rover Triumph, run by Ray Horrocks and William Pratt Thompson (an American), respectively. Bob Knight is made managing director of 'Jaguar Cars' within 'JRT', with the following

Jaguar men alongside him on the board: Mike Beasley (manufacturing), David Fielden (vehicle quality), Harry Mundy (power units) and Jim Randle (vehicle engineering). At a Jaguar Cars meeting on 28 August it is recorded that concept approval for the **XJ40** is planned for next March. Jaguar engineering continues to be understaffed, and at the October board meeting Mundy stresses the 'urgent need to improve grading and salaries in engineering'.

1979:   Although he is managing director, Bob Knight continues to occupy his engineering offices, while Pratt Thompson uses Jaguar's front offices to run JRT. On 29 January, Mike Beasley warns the Jaguar board of growing problems in maintaining paint quality during a switch to new paint processes and a paint shop away from Browns Lane, but expresses long-term confidence that the Castle Bromwich factory will eventually produce metal and paint finishes 'to a satisfactory quality'. Bob Knight states Jaguar's 'determination to achieve high quality standards from the start of Series Three' (the second XJ facelift, the launch of which has been postponed from autumn 1978 to spring 1979). At February's meeting, it is decided to divorce the 'slant-six' power unit from the vehicle project 'to ensure that the engine proceeds as quickly as possible' — if necessary ahead of **XJ40**, for which 'ease of manufacture' is now considered as the priority. Also in February, Jim Randle publishes a highly technical concept paper on sports cars of the future. (Is this the true birth of XJ41?)

In April, Bob Knight says that Pressed Steel-Fisher, Swindon, want 'another three months' delay' on the **XJ40** body. In June, Beasley reports that current-model body quality from PS-F is 'totally unacceptable', with a very high incidence of poor metalwork. Browns Lane's facilities are incapable of handling the volume of 're-working'. Output slumps to loss-making levels and it is realized that the difficulties are fundamental; it is agreed that a solution must be found and the problem is assigned to Jim Randle and Mike Beasley. At the same meeting it is noted that the Borg Warner 85 transmission is under development and that a diesel engine is to be included in the **XJ40** concept. Another

meeting is scheduled for 28 August, but does not appear to have been held.

Production falls to its lowest level for more than twenty years. Pratt Thompson leaves JRT, which is disbanded. Subsequently, Sir Michael Edwardes describes JRT as 'really only a holding company with Rover and Triumph still separate identities in the minds of many managers and employees, and with Jaguar, quite rightly, looking for greater independence'. Edwardes tries unsuccessfully to recruit John Egan from Massey-Ferguson and a BL executive, Percy Plant, is appointed as temporary chairman of Jaguar.

1980:   In January, BL board approval is given to a £32.2 million investment in the new January AJ6 engines. At a meeting on 31 January Percy Plant reports that BL views have, however, 'hardened' on the need for a diesel engine by 1984. The BL Cars Programme Review Committee's firm view is passed on for Knight's attention, ie. that the **XJ40** programme volumes are not achievable without a suitable diesel version and that the volumes should therefore be reduced or a diesel project brought forward. Under 'Any Other Business' Beasley reports that the order for £5 million-worth of AJ6 cylinder block machining equipment is to go to the British firm Kearney and Trecker. There is a general 'buy British' campaign as sales continue to slump while quality problems remain. Harry Mundy (power unit chief) retires in March; Bob Knight leaves Mundy's farewell party early because of an urgent meeting with Percy Plant. In that month, after due consideration, John Egan accepts a renewed invitation to run Jaguar. Also in the month of March, the Department of Industry approves the proposed AJ6 engine investment, as Trevor Crisp becomes chief power-unit engineer in succession to Mundy.

John Egan chairs his first board meeting at Browns Lane on 17 April, when he confirms that he has taken over from Percy Plant, and expresses his 'considerable faith' in Jaguar. On 26 and 27 April, Egan declares his commitment to Jaguar, and brings to an end a potentially crippling strike over grading. Egan's position as *managing* director as well as chairman becomes clear when Bob Knight (61) negotiates early retirement in July. Jim Randle's position as engineering overlord is

Sir John Egan, M.Sc., B.Sc.Econ., FIC, Hon. D.Sc., Chairman and Chief Executive of Jaguar plc.

thus clarified, too. The BL board approves the **XJ40** concept submission on 9 July.

At the August Jaguar board meeting, Jim Randle reports that the Italian VM 3.6-litre diesel installed in Series Three is basically sound but badly installed and in need of a better converter match. Two 3.8-litre diesels are on order, and production is being considered for 1982. Discussion points at the September meeting include a workforce reduction and the early operations of a quality task force. Use of the AJ6 engine in the XJ-S is timed for spring 1983 at this stage, whereas launch of the **XJ40** 'has been slipped six months to 1984'. (With hindsight this was a positive decision, since Jaguar was determined that the new car should be right first time. Later 'slippages' were much less worrying, since the company was running, profitably, with existing models taking on a new lease of life.)

In October, purchase director Pat Audrain stresses the need to reconsider the alternatives of General Motors' automatic gearbox and the ZF unit, which is being offered for £75 less. At this meeting it is reported that the interior design for **XJ40** is going well and that two XJ-Ss have been converted to take the 3.6-litre AJ6 engine.

The most recent board meeting minutes to be made available for study are those dated 26 November 1980, reporting that seven of the top twenty quality problems have been resolved, and that the rest will be surmounted by July 1981.

Following drastic action to put Jaguar's house in order — largely through gaining exclusive use of and investment in the Castle Bromwich paint plant — production remains well below economic levels, and a loss of £52.2 million after tax is later calculated for the financial year, which now coincides with the calendar year. However, there is light at the end of the tunnel as Randle prepares the **XJ40** 'Engineering Status' brochure for presentation to BL and the Government.

1981: In February the BL board approves the £77.92 million investment programme to put the **XJ40** on the road. The Department of Industry adds its seal of approval in April, and the new Jaguar is no longer just a dream. Jaguar's serious intentions are conveyed to all concerned — notably the US trade — through roadshows, presentations, and demonstrations of the effect of Japanese-style 'quality circles' and other new incentives on existing models. XJ-S production is virtually halted, but returns in strength in the autumn with the 'HE' models which feature modified combustion chambers (a Michael May patent) and other improvements. Dedication to the future means an all-time low production figure (less than 14,000 cars in the year), but stringent economy measures reduce the final loss figure for the twelve months to £36.3 million. Jaguar 'bottoms out'.

1982: [*More detailed information on the period since early 1982 can be found elsewhere in this book, notably in Chapter 6.*] The setting up of sales, marketing, and public affairs departments virtually completes the restoration of autonomy to Jaguar, just a decade after the retirement of Sir William Lyons who, at eighty, is still honorary president and the valued confidant of Egan and Randle. Production soars to some 22,000 cars and an operating profit of £10.1 million

permits a final 'plus' figure, after tax, of £6.5 million. A record number of cars (over 10,000) is sold in the USA. At home 'Jaguar Cars Ltd', reg. no. 1672070, is incorporated once again on 15 October. At the same time, other associated companies are created, including the non-trading 'Jaguar Cars Holdings Ltd', reg. no. 1672066.

1983: On New Year's Day, an agreement (dated 23 December 1982) takes effect, whereby Jaguar acquires from BL Cars all aspects of business relating to vehicles sold under the marque names Jaguar and Daimler. At the same time Jaguar Cars Inc (USA) and Jaguar Canada Inc — formerly subsidiaries of BL — become part of the new Jaguar Group, still run by Graham Whitehead and John Mackie respectively, with the former responsible for all North American operations. The XJR-5 — a Jaguar V12-powered mid-engined prototype built by Group 44 Inc in Virginia — wins four events in the International Motor Sports Association (IMSA) Camel GT prototype race series as part of the US sales and marketing campaign. Group 44 chief Bob Tullius is runner-up in this championship and over 15,000 Jaguars are sold in North America this year. In Jaguar's second full year back in motor sports, Tom Walkinshaw is runner-up in the European Touring Car Championship; his company,

Sir John Egan meets Jaguar's longest-serving agent, Emil Frey, who signed his first Swallow contract in 1926. With them are Jaguar's John Morgan and Walter Frey, now the head of the Zurich-based empire founded by his father.

TWR, prepares XJ-S cars which are sponsored by Motul Oil and Jaguar Cars. The XJ-S cabriolet and the AJ6 engine (now 3.6 litres rather than 3.8) are launched simultaneously in the autumn. The year shows increased production (over 27,000 cars) and profits of £49.5 million after tax. John Egan receives several accolades, notably Midlander of the Year. For the British government, Norman Tebbit confirms that Jaguar will be sold privately by the nationalized BL company.

1984: This is the year of consolidation. On behalf of BLMC Ltd (a wholly-owned subsidiary of BL plc), Hill Samuel offers for sale 177,880,000 ordinary shares of 25p each at 165p per share. The remaining 2,120,000 shares (out of 180 million) are retained to be made available to the trustees of the Jaguar Employee Share Scheme at the same price. The ordinary shares are listed at the London Stock Exchange in early August. Jaguar plc is formed, reg. no. 1672066, formerly Jaguar Cars Holdings. Directors are John Egan, Mike Beasley, John Edwards, Ken Edwards and Graham Whitehead — *plus* non-executive board members Edward Bond (CBI), Ray Horrocks (BL) and Hamish Orr-Ewing (Jaguar plc chairman for the 'privatization' period). The executive management committee (ie, Jaguar Cars Ltd operations board) consists of John Egan (chief executive), Pat Audrain (purchasing), Mike Beasley (manufacturing), David Boole (communications and public affairs), John Edwards (finance), Ken Edwards (personnel and also company secretary), David Fielden (quality), Neil Johnson (sales and marketing), Jim Randle (engineering), and Graham Whitehead (North America).

Group 44's XJR-5 wins the Miami Grand

Prix and brings Jaguar back to Le Mans. TWR XJ-S coupés win many European events including the 24-hour endurance race at Spa-Francorchamps in the Belgian Ardennes; Tom Walkinshaw is European Touring Car race champion — the first Jaguar driver to take this title for twenty-one years. Jaguar acquires these non-trading companies to preserve their historic names: The Daimler Company Ltd, Daimler Transport Vehicles Ltd, SS Cars Ltd, and the Lanchester Motor Company Ltd. The continued success of the Series Three (*c.* 27,500) and the XJ-S (*c.* 6,000) makes 1984 an all-time record year for production (over 33,000 cars); profits are £91.5 million (or £42.6 million after tax). Retained profits of £55.5 million are slightly up on 1983 (£55.4 million).

1985: Jaguar's honorary president and founder, Sir William Lyons, RDI, DTech, FRSA, Hon FIMechE, dies on 8 February, aged eighty-three. Jaguar plc board members are the same as in 1984, except that Sir John Pearce joins as non-executive director while Ray Horrocks and Hamish Orr-Ewing stand down. Jaguar Cars Ltd directors remain unchanged. Sponsored by the respective Jaguar importers, there are major race wins by Group 44 at Road Atlanta, Georgia (XJR-5), and by TWR at Bathurst, Australia (XJ-S). The World Sports-Prototype Championship series draws to a close with a second place for the new TWR-built mid-engined XJR-6 in the Selangor 500-mile race. Some 38,000 cars are produced — over 20,000 being destined for the USA — and pre-tax profits go up to £121.3 million for the year (£87.6 million after tax).

1986: Lady Greta, widow of Sir William Lyons, dies aged eighty-four. In June, John Egan receives the accolade of a knighthood from HM the Queen (Birthday Honours list). The Jaguar plc

and Jaguar Cars Ltd boards remain the same as in 1985, except that former Lotus executive Roger Putman is appointed director of sales and marketing in place of Neil Johnson, who retains an advisory role while returning to serve in HM Forces (where he had begun his career). In racing, the TWR XJR-6 and Group 44 XJR-7 score their first victories at Silverstone, England, and Daytona, USA, respectively.

Jim Randle and his engineering staff give the **XJ40** its first technical preview at the Institution of Mechanical Engineers, London, in August. Press reviews in Scotland follow throughout September. The **XJ40** is announced to the public on 8 October. Randle receives the UDT/Guild of Motoring Writers' 'Top Car' Award for the **XJ40** in November. Jaguar production for the year surpasses 41,000 cars, despite the switch to new models. 1986 pre-tax profits are, once again, over £120m, and show the effect of this switch, plus further much needed investment.

1987: Sir John Egan's avowed intent is to continue to propel the company onward and upward at the rate of 10 to 15 per cent per annum. (The plan includes building and selling over 50,000 cars this year.) Manufacturing and vehicle engineering facilities are financed from within, and modernized in line with their remarkable achievements. A self-contained vehicle engineering centre at Whitley, Coventry, is completed and occupied during the year, as future design plans are laid. On the sporting front, after many successes, the ultimate goal is still to achieve outright victory in the 24-hour race at Le Mans, an event last won by a Jaguar exactly thirty years before.

The Silk Cut Jaguar team takes the lead in the World Sports Car Championship, the new mid-engined XJR-8 prototype winning the

Intensifying the image: designed by Tony Southgate, built for Jaguar by Tom Walkinshaw Racing Ltd and driven by John Watson, Jan Lammers, Eddie Cheever and Raul Boesel, the XJR-8 swept all before it in early 1987 — adding to the impetus of the XJ40 launch. This picture, taken at Silverstone in May, shows the V12 mid-engined cars en route to their fourth successive victory.

Road and race versions of the XK engine, born in 1948 and still in limited production (for Daimler limousine and military use) four decades later, although now replaced by the AJ6 units for the Jaguar XJ40 range. Well over 700,000 XK-engined cars had been produced by the time the Series 3 XJ6 was phased out in April 1987.

first four rounds at Jarama, Jerez, Monza and Silverstone — *and* making the best time of all the participants at the pre-Le Mans test session in late May (thirty years have passed since a Jaguar last won the 24-hour French classic). Watson/Lammers (Jaguar) lead Derek Bell/Hans-Joachim Stuck (Porsche) by one point, with Cheever/Boesel (Jaguar) close behind at this stage of the drivers' championship. Jaguar leads the works Porsche team easily in the team title chase......but there's still a long way to go.

In the USA, Group 44 scores its eighth outright IMSA victory when the XJR-7 of Hurley Haywood and John Morton wins the Los Angeles Times 'Gran Prix' from the favourite — the Porsche 962 of Chip Robinson and Al Holbert. This, however, fails to prevent the issue in early May of a press announcement to the effect that Tom Walkinshaw is to take over Jaguar's racing programme not only for Group C but for IMSA GTP activity in 1988. Jaguar wants one racing team, not two, and it chooses the one with the better record in terms of technology,

outside sponsorship and (over the past five years at least) results.

The first four months of 1987 show that 15,186 Jaguars and Daimlers have been despatched, as opposed to 14,690 in the equivalent period of 1986, but there is an **XJ40** recall in May: a supplier fails to meet his commitment, so foreign bodies in the fluid lead to a loss of servo-assistance in the brakes. No total failures are recorded and the problem is not allowed to affect the North American market at all — but Egan is quick to contain the situation. He calls on all involved to achieve 'an even higher level of diligence' and reminds the whole Jaguar workforce that 'quality is the key to our success'. By June, mercurial 'whizz-kid' Derek Waelend is pursuing his career with Lotus, having seen Jaguar's new manufacturing processes through from mid-1983 to the **XJ40** launch on the American market four years later. Assistant Managing Director Mike Beasley continues to lead the Jaguar manufacturing team, however, and, although the projected target of 50,000 cars becomes a more realistic

Jaguar AJ6 engine in 2.9-litre form.

Evolution of the species: an XJ40 meets its ancestors, a group of Swallow-bodied Austins, on the occasion of their Diamond Jubilee. The Austin Seven Swallow was announced on 20 May 1927.

47,000, Jaguar looks set for another record year in 1987 despite the state of the US dollar.

On 19 May, Jim Randle receives the Sir William Lyons Trophy for his services to Jaguar engineering and the XJ40 in particular. Wednesday 20 May marks the Diamond Jubilee of (Sir) William Lyons' original car announcement, that of the Austin Swallow — the first four-wheeler of the species. And there are accolades galore for Jaguar and its new XJ6 — including a Queen's Award for Technology and the AA Gold Medal.

John Mackie, head of Jaguar's Canadian operation, with Graham Whitehead (left) and Sir John Egan at the Tampa, Florida, dealer conference, Spring 1987.